New Rules for the New Economy

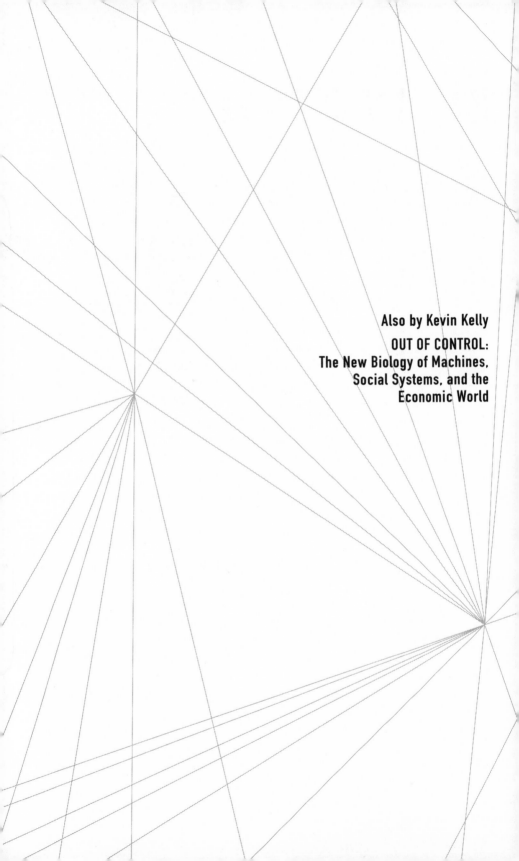

Also by Kevin Kelly

OUT OF CONTROL:
The New Biology of Machines,
Social Systems, and the
Economic World

KEVIN KELLY

New Rules

for the

New Economy

10 RADICAL STRATEGIES FOR A CONNECTED WORLD

VIKING

VIKING
Published by the Penguin Group
Penguin Putnam Inc., 375 Hudson Street,
New York, New York 10014, U.S.A.
Penguin Books Ltd, 27 Wrights Lane,
London W8 5TZ, England
Penguin Books Australia Ltd, Ringwood,
Victoria, Australia
Penguin Books Canada Ltd, 10 Alcorn Avenue,
Toronto, Ontario, Canada M4V 3B2
Penguin Books (N.Z.) Ltd, 182–190 Wairau Road,
Auckland 10, New Zealand
Penguin India, 210 Chiranjiv Tower, 43 Nehru Place,
New Delhi 11009, India

Penguin Books Ltd. Registered Offices:
Harmondsworth, Middlesex, England

First published in 1998 by Viking Penguin,
a member of Penguin Putnam Inc.

10   9

A portion of this work first appeared in *Wired*, September 1997,
as "New Rules for the New Economy: Twelve Dependable
Principles for Thriving in a Turbulent World."

LIBRARY OF CONGRESS CATALOGING-IN-PUBLICATION DATA
Kelly, Kevin.
New rules for the new economy : 10 radical strategies for
a connected world / Kevin Kelly.
p.   cm.
Includes bibliographical references and index.
ISBN 0–670–88111–2
1. Economic forecasting.   2. Business forecasting.   I. Title
HC59 15.K45   1998
658—dc21   98–36917

This book is printed on acid-free paper.
(∞)

Printed in the United States of America
Set in Electra
Designed by Francesca Belanger

For Gia-Miin

CONTENTS

New Rules for the New Economy

This New Economy

No one can escape the transforming fire of machines. Technology, which once progressed at the periphery of culture, now engulfs our minds as well as our lives. Is it any wonder that technology triggers such intense fascination, fear, and rage?

One by one, each of the things that we care about in life is touched by science and then altered. Human expression, thought, communication, and even human life have been infiltrated by high technology. As each realm is overtaken by complex techniques, the usual order is inverted, and new rules established. The mighty tumble, the once confident are left desperate for guidance, and the nimble are given a chance to prevail.

But while the fast-forward technological revolution gets all the headlines these days, something much larger is slowly turning beneath it. Steadily driving the gyrating cycles of cool technogadgets and gotta-haves is an emerging new economic order. The geography of wealth is being reshaped by our tools. We now live in a new economy created by shrinking computers and expanding communications.

This new economy represents a tectonic upheaval in our commonwealth, a far more turbulent reordering than mere digital hardware has produced. The new economic order has its own distinct opportunities and pitfalls. If past economic transformations are any guide, those who play by the new rules will prosper, while those who ignore them will not. We have seen only the beginnings of the anxiety, loss, excitement, and gains that many people will experience as our world shifts to a new highly technical planetary economy.

This new economy has three distinguishing characteristics: It is global. It favors intangible things—ideas, information, and relationships. And it is intensely interlinked. These three attributes produce a new type of marketplace and society, one that is rooted in ubiquitous electronic networks.

Networks have existed in every economy. What's different now is that networks, enhanced and multiplied by technology, penetrate our lives so deeply that "network" has become the central metaphor around which our thinking and our economy are organized. Unless we can understand the distinctive logic of networks, we can't profit from the economic transformation now under way.

New Rules for the New Economy lays out ten essential dynamics of this emerging financial order. These rules are fundamental principles that are hardwired into this new territory, and that apply to all businesses and industries, not just high-tech ones. Think of the principles outlined in this book as rules of thumb.

Like any rules of thumb they aren't infallible. Instead, they act as beacons charting out general directions. They are designed to illuminate deep-rooted forces that will persist into the first half of the next century. These ten laws attempt to capture the underlying principles that shape our new economic environment, rather than chase current short-term business trends.

The key premise of this book is that the principles governing the world of the soft—the world of intangibles, of media, of software, and of services—will soon command the world of the hard—the world of reality, of atoms, of objects, of steel and oil, and the hard work done by the sweat of brows. Iron and lumber will obey the laws of software, automobiles will follow the rules of networks, smokestacks will comply with the decrees of knowledge. If you want to envision where the future of your industry will be, imagine it as a business built entirely around the soft, even if at this point you see it based in the hard.

Of course, all the mouse clicks in the world can't move atoms in real space without tapping real energy, so there are limits to how far the soft will infiltrate the hard. But the evidence everywhere indicates that the hard world is irreversibly softening. Therefore one can gain a huge advantage simply by riding this conversion. To stay ahead, you chiefly need to understand how the soft world works—how networks prosper and grow, how interfaces control attention, how plentitude drives value—and then apply those principles to the hard world of now.

The tricks of the intangible trade will become the tricks of your trade.

The new economy deals in wispy entities such as information, relationships, copyright, entertainment, securities, and derivatives. The U.S. economy is already demassifying, drifting toward these intangibles. The creations most in demand from the United States (those exported) lost 50% of their physical weight per dollar of value in only six years. The disembodied world of computers, entertainment, and telecommunications is now an industry larger than any of the old giants of yore, such as construction, food products, or automobile manufacturing. This new information-based sector already occupies 15% of the total U.S. economy.

Yet digital bits, stock options, copyright, and brands have no measurable economic shape. What is the unit of software: Floppy disks? Lines of code? Number of programs? Number of features? Economists are baffled. Walter Wriston, former chairman of Citicorp, likes to grumble that federal economists can tell us exactly how many left-handed cowboys are employed each year, yet have no idea how many software programs are in use. The dials on our economic dashboard have started spinning wildly, blinking and twittering as we head into new territory. It's possible the gauges are all broken, but it is much more likely the world is turning upside down.

Remember GM? In the 1950s business reporters were infatuated with General Motors. GM was the paragon of industrial progress. It not only made cars, it made America. GM was the richest company on earth. To many intelligent observers, GM was the future of business in general. It was huge, and bigger was better. It was stable and paternal, providing lifetime employment. It controlled all parts of its vast empire, ensuring quality and high profits. GM was the best, and when the pundits looked ahead 40 years they imagined all successful companies would be like GM.

How ironic that ever since the future has arrived, GM is now the counter example. Today, if your company is like GM, it's in deep trouble.

Instead, pundits point to Microsoft. Microsoft is the role model. It is the highest-valued company on Earth. It produces intangibles. It rides the logic of standards. Its sky-high stock valuation reflects the new productivity. So we look ahead and say: In 40 years all companies will be like Microsoft.

History would suggest this is a bad bet. The obvious lesson is that we tend to project the future from what's fashionable at present. Right now software and entertainment companies are very profitable, so we assume they are role models. Brad DeLong, an economist at UC Berkeley, has a handy theory of economic history. He says that various sectors of economy wax and wane in prominence like movie stars. The history of the American economy can be seen as a parade of "heroic" industries that first appear on the scene as unknowns, then heroically "save" the economy by doing economic miracles, and for a time are treated as economic stars. In the 1900s, the automobile industry was heroic: There was incredible innovation, many, many car company upstarts, incredible productivity. It was a wild and exciting time. But then the heroism died away and the auto industry became big, monolithic, boring, and hugely profitable. In DeLong's view, the latest heroic savior is the information, communication, and entertainment complex. Businesses in the realm of software and communications are now valorous: They pull successes out of a hat, stack up unending innovation, and perform economic miracles. Long live computers!

There is a lot of common sense to DeLong's view of heroic industry. Just because Microsoft is heroic now, doesn't mean all companies will follow their lead and replicate intellectual property on floppy disks with a profit margin of 90%. No doubt many, many companies in the future will not resemble Microsoft at all. Somebody has to fix the plugged toilets of the world, somebody has to build houses, somebody has to drive the trucks hauling our milk.

Even *Wired* magazine, mouthpiece of the digital revolution—where I serve as one of the editors—does not approach the ideal of an intangible company. *Wired* is located smack in the middle of an old-fashioned downtown city, and in one year turns 8 million pounds (or 48 railway cars) of dried tree pulp, and 330,000 pounds of bright colored ink into hard copies of the magazine. A lot of atoms are involved.

So how can we make the claim that *all* businesses in the world will be reshaped by advances in chips and glass fibers and spectrum? What makes this particular technological advance so special? Why is the business hero of this moment so much more important than its recent predecessors?

Because communication—which in the end is what the digital technology and media are all about—is not just a sector of the economy. Communication *is* the economy.

This vanguard is not about computers. Computers are over. Most of the consequences that we can expect from computers as stand-alone machines have already happened. They have sped up our lives, and made managing words, numbers, and pixels quite extraordinary, but they have not had much more effect beyond that.

The new economy is about *communication*, deep and wide. All the transformations suggested in this book stem from the fundamental way we are revolutionizing communications. Communication is the foundation of society, of our culture, of our humanity, of our own individual identity, and of all economic systems. This is why networks are such a big deal. Communication is so close to culture and society itself that the effects of technologizing it are beyond the scale of a mere industrial-sector cycle. Communication, and its ally computers, is a special case in economic history. Not because it happens to be the fashionable leading business sector of our day, but because its cultural, technological, and conceptual impacts reverberate at the root of our lives.

Certain technologies (such as the integrated circuit chip) spur innovation and novelty in other technologies; these catalysts are called "enabling technologies." Occasionally an economic sector will leverage power and accelerate the advance of other sectors in an economy. These can be thought of as "enabling sectors." Computer chips and communication networks have produced a sector of an economy that is transforming all the other sectors.

Only a relatively small number of people have ever been directly employed in the world of finance. Yet ever since the days of the Venetian bankers, financial innovations such as mortgages, insurance, venture funding, stocks, checks, credit cards, mutual funds, to name only a few, have completely reshaped our economy. They have enabled the rise of corporations, of market capitalism, of the industrial age, and much more. Unlike many previous heroic industries such as the electrical power industry or the chemical industry, this small sector has influenced how all business is done, and how we structure our lives.

As tremendous as the influence of financial inventions have been, the influence of network inventions will be as great, or greater.

It took several billion years on Earth for unicellular life to evolve. And it took another billion years or so for that single-celled life to evolve multicellular arrangements—each cell touching a few cells near it to make a living spherical organism. At first, the sphere was the only form multicellular life could take because its cells had to be near one another to coordinate their functions. After another billion years, life eventually evolved the first cellular neuron—a thin strand of tissue—which enabled two cells to communicate over a distance. With that single enabling innovation, the variety of life boomed. With neurons, life no longer had to remain bounded in a blob. It was possible to arrange cells into almost any shape, size, and function. Butterflies, orchids, and kangaroos all became possible. Life quickly exploded in a million different unexpected ways, into fantastic awesome varieties, until wonderful life was everywhere.

Silicon chips linked into high-bandwidth channels are the neurons of our culture. Until this moment, our economy has been in the multicellular stage. Our industrial age has required each customer or company to almost physically touch one another. Our firms and organizations resemble blobs. Now, by the enabling invention of silicon and glass neurons, a million new forms are possible. Boom! An infinite variety of new shapes and sizes of social organizations are suddenly possible. Unimaginable forms of commerce can now coalesce in this new economy. We are about to witness an explosion of entities built on relationships and technology that will rival the early days of life on Earth in their variety.

In the future very few companies will look like Microsoft, or even *Wired*. Even ancient forms will be bent. Farming, and trucking, plumbing, and other traditional occupations will continue, just as unicellular life continues. But the economics of farmers and friends, in their own way, will obey the logic of networks, just as Microsoft does now.

We see evidence for that already. A farmer in America—the hero of the agricultural economy—rides in a portable office on his tractor. It's air conditioned, has a phone, a satellite-driven GPS location device, and sophisticated sensors near the ground. At home his computer is connected to the never-ending stream of weather data, the worldwide grain markets, his bank, moisture detectors in the soil, digitized maps, and his own spreadsheets of cash flow. Yes, he gets dirt under his fingernails, but his manual labor takes place in the context of a network economy.

Much the same can be said about truck drivers. While the experience of sitting behind a wheel remains unchanged, the new tools of trucking—bar codes, radios, dispatch algorithms, route hubs, and even roads themselves—all follow the logic of networks. Thus, the very sweat of truckers as they manually load and unload heavy boxes becomes incorporated into the network economy.

Our economy is an amalgamation of diverse styles of trade, commerce, and social exchanges. New economic functions develop around the operating old. Barter, one of the earliest forms of commerce, has not gone away. The barter economy ran through the agricultural age, the industrial age, and continues today. Indeed most of what happens on the World Wide Web is barter. Even many years from now a significant portion of what the economy does will be done by the industrial layers—machines churning out goods and moving materials. The old economies will continue to operate profitably within the deep cortex of the new economy.

Yet the inertia of the industrial age continues to mesmerize us. Between 1990 and 1996 the number of people making tangible things—stuff you can drop on your toe—decreased by 1%, while the number of people employed in providing "services" (intangibles) grew 15%. Presently a mere 18% of U.S. employment is in manufacturing. But three quarters of those 18% actually perform network economy jobs while working for a manufacturing company. Instead of pushing atoms they push bits around: accountants, researchers, designers, marketing, sales, lawyers, and all the rest who sit at a desk. Only a minuscule percentage of the workforce performs industrial age tasks, yet our politics, our media, our funding, and our education continue the grand fantasy that industrial jobs need to be created. Within a generation, two at the most, the number of people working in honest-to-goodness manufacturing jobs will be no more than the number of farmers in the land—less than a few percent. Far more than we realize it, the network economy is pulling in everyone.

As the world of chips and glass fibers and wireless waves goes, so goes the rest of the world.

In the face of history this bold assertion may seem naive. But every once in a while something big and new does happen. It must have felt that way to the home-craft Luddites who sensed that the industrial age was not just about newfangled looms, but foreshadowed deep, systemic changes with life-changing ramifications. Were they naive to think that machines would ultimately transform the ancient and holy act of planting seeds and harvesting the grain? Of breeding cows? Of the structure of communities?

"Listen to the technology," advises Carver Mead, one of the inventors of the modern computer chip. "Find out what it is telling you." Following that lead, I have assembled these rules of thumb by asking these questions: How do our tools shape our destiny? What kind of an economy is our new technology suggesting?

Steel ingots and rivers of oil, smokestacks and factory lines, and even tiny seeds and cud-chewing cows are all becoming enmeshed in the world of smart chips and fast bandwidth, and sooner or later they will begin to fully obey the new rules of the new economy, as everything will. I've listened to the technology, and as best as I can determine, the technology repeats ten distinct refrains, as premiered in the following ten chapters.

1 EMBRACE THE SWARM
The Power of Decentralization

The atom is the icon of the 20th century. The atom whirls alone. It is the metaphor for individuality. But the atom is the past. The symbol for the next century is the net. The net has no center, no orbits, no certainty. It is an indefinite web of causes. The net is the archetype displayed to represent all circuits, all intelligence, all interdependence, all things economic, social, or ecological, all communications, all democracy, all families, all large systems, almost all that we find interesting and important. Whereas the atom represents clean simplicity, the net channels messy complexity.

The net is our future.

Of all the endeavors we humans are now engaged in, perhaps the grandest of them all is the steady weaving together of our lives, minds, and artifacts into a global scale network. This great work has been going on for decades, but recently our ability to connect has accelerated. Two brand-new technological achievements—the silicon chip and the silicate glass fiber—have rammed together with incredible speed. Like nuclear particles crashing together in a cyclotron, the intersection of these two innovations has unleashed a never-before-seen force: the power of a pervasive net. As this grand net spreads, an animated swarm is reticulating the surface of the planet. We are clothing the globe with a network society.

The dynamic of our society, and particularly our new economy, will increasingly obey the logic of networks. Understanding how

networks work will be the key to understanding how the economy works.

Any network has two ingredients: nodes and connections. In the grand network we are now assembling, the size of the nodes is collapsing while the quantity and quality of the connections are exploding. These two physical realms, the collapsing microcosm of silicon and the exploding telecosm of connections, form the matrix through which the new economy of ideas flows.

A single silicon transistor today can only be seen in a microscope. In a few years it will take a microscope to see an entire chip of transistors. As the size of silicon chips shrinks to the microscopic, their costs shrink to the microscopic as well. In 1950 a transistor cost five dollars. Today it costs one hundredth of a cent. In 2003 one transistor will cost a microscopic nanocent. A chip with a billion transistors will eventually cost only a few cents.

What this means is that chips are becoming cheap and tiny enough to slip into *every object we make*. Eventually, every can of soup will have a chip on its lid. Every light switch will contain a chip. Every book will have a chip embedded in its spine. Every shirt will have at least one chip sewn into its hem. Every item on a grocery shelf will have stuck to it, or embedded within itself, a button of silicon. There are 10 trillion objects manufactured in the world each year and the day will come when each one of them will carry a flake of silicon.

This is not crazy, nor distant. Ten years ago the notion that all doors in a building should contain a computer chip seemed ludicrous, but now there is hardly a hotel door in the U.S. without a blinking, beeping chip in its lock. These microscopic chips will be so cheap we'll throw them away. Thin slices of plastic known as smart cards now hold a throwaway chip smart enough to be your banker. If National Semiconductor gets its way, soon every FedEx package will be stamped with a disposable silicon flake that smartly tracks the contents of the package on its journey. And if an ephemeral envelope can have a chip, so can your chair, each bag of candy, a new coat, a basketball. Soon, all manufactured objects, from sneakers to drill presses to lamp shades to cans of soda, will contain a tiny sliver of embedded thought.

And why not?

Today the world is populated by 200 million computers. Andy Grove of Intel happily estimates that we'll see 500 million computers by 2002. Yet for every expensive chip put into a beige computer box, there are now 30 other cheap processors put into everyday things. The number of non-computer chips already pulsating in the world is 6 billion—one chip for every human on Earth.

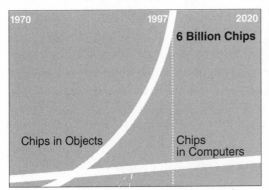

We are moving from crunching to connecting. While the number of computer chips is rising, the number of chips in objects other than computers is rising faster.

You already have a non-PC chip embedded in your car and stereo and rice cooker and phone. These chips are dumb chips, with limited ambitions. A chip in your car's brakes doesn't have to do floating-point math, spreadsheets, or video processing; it only needs to brake like a bulldog.

Because they have limited functions and can be produced in great quantity, these dumb chips are ultracheap to make. One industry observer calculated that an embedded processor chip costs less to manufacture than a ball bearing. Since they can be stamped out as fast and cheap as candy gumdrops, these chips are known in the trade as "jelly beans." Dumb, cheap jelly bean chips are invading the world far faster than PCs did.

This is not surprising. You can only use one or two personal computers at a time, but the number of other objects in your life is almost unlimited. First, we'll put jelly bean chips into high-tech appliances, then later into all tools, and then eventually into all objects. If current rates continue there'll be some 10 billion tiny grains of silicon chips embedded into our environment by 2005.

Putting a dot of intelligence into every object we make at first gives us a billion dimwitted artifacts. But we are also, at the same time, connecting these billion nodes, one by one.

We are connecting everything to everything.

There is something mysterious that happens when we take large numbers of things that are fairly limited and connect them all together. When we take the dumb chip in each cash register in a store and link them into a swarm, we have something more than dumb. We have real-time buying patterns that can manage inventory. If we take the dumb chips that already regulate the guts of an automobile engine, and let them communicate an engine's performance to the mechanic of a trucking firm, those dumb chips can smartly cut expensive road repairs. (Mercedes Benz recently announced it is planning to embed a web server into its top-of-the-line model cars so technicians can spot service problems remotely.) When connected into a swarm, small thoughts become smart.

When we permit any object to transmit a small amount of data and to receive input from its neighborhood, we change an inert object into an animated node.

It is not necessary that each connected object transmit much data. A tiny chip plastered inside a water tank on an Australian ranch transmits only the telegraphic 2-bit message of whether the tank is FULL or NOT. A chip attached to the ear of each steer on the same ranch beams out his location in GPS numbers; nothing more. "I'm here, I'm here" it tells the rancher's log book; nothing more. The chip in the gate at the end of the rancher's road communicates only a single word, reporting when it was last opened: "Tuesday."

It does not take sophisticated infrastructure to transmit these dumb bits. Stationary objects—parts of a building, tools on the factory floor, fixed cameras—are wired together. The nonstationary rest—that is, most manufactured objects—are linked by infrared and radio, creating a wireless web vastly larger than the wired web. The same everyday frequencies that run garage door openers and TV remote controls will be multiplied by the millions to carry the dumb messages of connected objects.

The glory of these connected crumbs is that they don't need to be individually sophisticated. They don't need speech recognition, artificial intelligence, or fancy expert systems. Instead, the network economy relies on the dumb power of bits linked together into a swarm.

Our brains tap into dumb power by clumping dumb neurons into consciousness. The internet banks on dumb power by connecting dumb personal computers. A personal computer is like a single brain neuron in a plastic box. When linked by the telecosm into a neural network, these dumb PC nodes create that fabulous intelligence called the World Wide Web.

Again and again we see the same dynamic at work in other domains: Dumb cells in our body work together in a swarm to produce an incredibly smart immune system, a system so sophisticated we still do not fully comprehend it.

Dumb parts, properly connected into a swarm, yield smart results.

A trillion dumb chips connected into a hive mind is the hardware. The software that runs through it is the network economy. A planet covered with hyperlinked chips is shrouded with waves of sensibility. Millions of moisture sensors in the fields of farmers shoot up data, hundreds of weather satellites beam down digitized images, thousands of cash registers spit out bit streams, myriad hospital bedside monitors trickle out signals, millions of web sites tally attention, and tens of millions of vehicles transmit their location code; all of this swirls into the web. That matrix of signals is the net.

The net is not just humans typing at one another on AOL, although that is a part of it and will be as long as seduction and flaming are enjoyable. Rather, the net is the total collective interaction of a trillion objects and living beings, linked together through air and glass.

This is the net that begets the network economy. According to MCI, data traffic on the global phone system will soon overtake voice traffic. The current total volume of voice traffic is 1,000 times that of data, but in three years that ratio will flip. ElectronicCast estimates data traffic—the talk of machines—will be ten times voice traffic by 2005. That means that by 2001 most of the signals zipping around the Earth will be machines talking to machines—file transfers, data streams, and the like. The network economy is already expanding to include new participants:

agents, bots, objects, and servers, as well as several billion more humans. We won't wait for AI to make intelligent systems; we'll do it with the swarm power of ubiquitous computing and pervasive connections.

The surest way to smartness is through massive dumbness.

The surest way to advance massive connectionism is to exploit decentralized forces—to link the distributed bottom. How do you build a better bridge? Let the parts talk to one another. How do you improve lettuce farming? Let the soil speak to the farmer's tractors. How do you make aircraft safe? Let the airplanes communicate among themselves and pick their own flight paths. This decentralized approach, known as "free flight," is a system the FAA is now trying to institute to increase safety and reduce air-traffic bottlenecks at airports.

Mathematical problems which were once intractable for supercomputers have been solved by using a swarm of small PCs. A very complex problem is broken up into tiny parts and distributed throughout the network. Likewise, vast research projects that would tax any one institution can be distributed to an ad hoc network. The Tree of Life is a worldwide taxonomic catalog of all living species on Earth administered on the web. Such a project is beyond the capabilities of one person or group. But a decentralized network can produce the necessary intelligence. Each local expert supplies their own data (on finches, or ferns or jellyfish) to fill in some of the blanks. As Larry Keely of the Doblin Group says, "No one is as smart as everyone."

Any process, even the bulkiest, most physical process, can be tackled by bottom-up swarm thinking. Take, for example, the delivery of wet cement in the less-than-digital economy of rural northern Mexico. Here Cemex (Cementos Mexicanos) runs a ready-mix cement business that is overwhelming its competitors and attracting worldwide interest. It used to be that getting a load of cement delivered on time to a construction site in the Guadalajara region was close to a miracle. Traffic delays, poor roads, contractors who weren't ready when they said they would be, all added up to an on-time delivery rate of less than 35%. In response, cement companies tried to enforce rigid advance reservations, which, when things went wrong (as they always did), only made matters worse ("Sorry, we can't reschedule you until next week.").

Cemex transformed the cement business by promising to deliver concrete faster than pizza. Using extensive networking technology—GPS real-time location signals from every truck, massive telecommunications throughout the company, and full information available to drivers and dispatchers, *with the authority to act on it*—the company was able to promise that if your load was more than 10 minutes late, you got a 20% discount.

Instead of rigidly trying to schedule everything ahead of time in an environment of chaos, Cemex let the drivers themselves schedule deliveries ad hoc and in real time. The drivers formed a flock of trucks crisscrossing the town. If a contractor called in an order for 12 yards of mix, the available truck closest to the site at that time would make the delivery. Dispatchers would ensure customer creditworthiness and guard against omissions, but the agents in the field had permission and the information they needed to schedule orders on the fly. Result: On-time delivery rates reached about 98%, with less wastage of hardened cement, and much happier customers.

Similar thinking has been used in a GM paint plant in Fort Wayne, Indiana. The wonderful choice of colors that customers now enjoy on new vehicles was playing havoc on the paint line. When one car after another is sprayed black, everything is easy. But when one car is red and the next white, the painting process is slowed down as painting equipment is cleansed of one color to make it ready for the next. (The clean-out procedure also wastes paint left in the paint lines.) Why not gang up all the white cars and do them together? Because ganging up slows the line. A car has to be built and completed as it is ordered, as quickly as possible. The solution embraces the swarm.

In the paint factory each robot painter (basically a dimwitted painting arm) is empowered to bid on a paint job. If it is currently painting red and a car slated to be red is coming down the assembly line, it says, "Let me do it," and it beckons the car to its paint station. The robots schedule their own work. They have very tiny brainlets, connected to a server. No central brain coordinates; the schedule comes from the swarm of minibrains. The result: GM saves $1.5 million a year. The equipment requires less paint (due to less cleaning between cars), and keeps the line moving faster.

Railways are now employing swarm technology. Centralized traffic control doesn't work when the traffic becomes very complex and time cycles are shortened. The Japanese use a bottom-up swarm model to schedule their famous bullet express trains, which boast incredible punctuality. Switching is done locally and autonomously as if the trains were a swarm with one mind. Railway owners in Houston are hoping to get a swarm model running for their rail yards. With their current centrally controlled system, the switching yards are so clogged that there is a permanent train of freight cars circling the greater Houston area as a buffer. It's like a mobile parking lot. When there's an opening in the yard, cars are pulled out of the holding pattern train. But with a system based on the swarm model, local lines can autonomously switch themselves, using minimal intelligence onboard. Such a self-regulating and self-optimizing system would reduce delays.

That's how the internet handles its amazing loads of traffic. Every email message is broken into bits, with each bit addressed in an envelope, and then all the fragmentary envelopes are sent into a global web of pathways. Each envelope seeks the quickest route it can find instant by instant. The email message becomes a swarm of bits that are reassembled at the other end into a unified message. If the message is re-sent to the same destination, the second time it may go by a wholly different route. Often the paths are inefficient. Your email may go to Timbuktu and back on its way across town. A centralized switching system would never direct messages in such a wasteful manner. But the inefficiencies of individual parts is overcome by the incredible reliability of the system as a whole.

The internet model has many lessons for the new economy but perhaps the most important is its embrace of dumb swarm power. The aim of swarm power is superior performance in a turbulent environment. When things happen fast and furious, they tend to route around central control. By interlinking many simple parts into a loose confederation, control devolves from the center to the lowest or outermost points, which collectively keep things on course.

A successful system, though, requires more than simply relinquishing control completely to the networked mob.

Complete surrender to the bottom is not what embracing swarm is about.

Let me retell a story that I told in *Out of Control*, a book that details the advantages, disadvantages, quirks, and consequences of complex systems governed by swarmlike processes. This story illustrates the power of a swarm, but it has a new ending, which shows how dumb power is not always enough.

In 1990 about 5,000 attendees at a computer graphics conference were asked to operate a computer flight simulator devised by Loren Carpenter. Each participant was connected into a network via a virtual joy stick. Each of the 5,000 copilots could move the plane's up/down, left/right controls as they saw fit, but the equipment was rigged so that the jet responded to the average decisions of the swarm of 5,000 participants. The flight took place in a large auditorium, so there was lateral communication (shouting) among the 5,000 copilots as they attempted to steer the plane. Remarkably, 5,000 novices were able to land a jet with almost no direction or coordination from above. One came away, as I did, convinced of the remarkable power of distributed, decentralized, autonomous, dumb control.

About five years after the first show (this is the update), Carpenter returned to the same conference with an improved set of simulations, better audience input controls, and greater expectations. This time, instead of flying a jet, the challenge was to steer a submarine through a 3D undersea world to capture some sea monster eggs. The same audience now had more choices, more dimensions, and more controls. The sub could go up/down, forward/back, open claws, close claws, and so on, with far more liberty than the jet had. When the audience first took command of the submarine, nothing happened. Audience members wiggled this control and that, shouted and counter-shouted instructions to one another, but nothing moved. Each person's instructions were being canceled by another person's orders. There was no cohesion. The sub didn't budge.

Finally Loren Carpenter's voice boomed from a loudspeaker in the back of the room. "Why don't you guys go to the right?" he hollered. Click! Instantly the sub zipped of to the right. With emergent coordination the audience adjusted the details of sailing and smoothly set off in search of sea monster eggs.

Loren Carpenter's voice was the voice of leadership. His short message carried only a few bits of information, but that tiniest speck of top-down control was enough to unleash the swarm below. He didn't steer the sub. The audience of 5,000 novice cocaptains did that very complicated maneuvering, magically and mysteriously. All Loren did was unlock the swarm's paralysis with a vision of where to aim. The swarm again figured out how to get there in the same marvelous way that they had figured out how to land the jet five years earlier.

Without some element of governance from the top, bottom-up control will freeze when options are many. Without some element of leadership, the many at the bottom will be paralyzed with choices.

Numerous small things connected together into a network generate tremendous power. But this swarm power will need some kind of minimal governance from the top to maximize its usefulness. Appropriate oversight depends on the network. In a firm, leadership is supervision; in social networks, government; in technical networks, standards and codes.

We have spent centuries obsessed with the role of top-down governance. Its importance remains. But the great excitement of the new economy is that we have only now begun to explore the power of the bottom, where peers holds sway. It is a vast mother lode waiting to be tapped. With the invention of a few distributed systems, such as the internet, we have merely probed the potential of what minimally centralized networks can do.

At present, there is far more to be gained by pushing the boundaries of what can be done by the bottom than by focusing on what can be done at the top.

When it comes to control, there is plenty of room at the bottom. What we are discovering is that peer-based networks with millions of parts, minimal oversight, and maximum connection among them can do far more than anyone ever expected. We don't yet know what the limits of decentralization are.

The great benefits reaped by the new economy in the coming decades will be due in large part to exploring and exploiting the power of decentralized and autonomous networks.

First we make a chip for every object. Then we connect them. We continue to connect all humans. We enlarge our conversation to include the world, and all its artifacts. We let the network of objects govern itself as much as possible; we add government where needed. In this matrix of connections, we interact and create. This is the net that is our future.

The whole process won't be completed by tomorrow, but the destiny is clear. We are connecting all to all, until we encompass the entire human-made world. And in that embrace is a new power.

Strategies

Move technology to invisibility. As technology becomes ubiquitous it also becomes invisible. The more chips proliferate, the less we will notice them. The more networking succeeds, the less we'll be aware of it.

In the early 1900s, at the heroic stage of the industrial economy, motors were changing the world. Big, heavy motors ran factories and trains and the gears of automation. If big motors changed work, they were sure to change the home, too. So the 1918 edition of the Sears, Roebuck catalog featured the Home Motor—a five-pound electrical beast that would "lighten the burden of the home." This single Home Motor would supply all the power needs of a modern family. Also for sale were plug-ins that attached to the central Home Motor: an egg beater device, a fan, a mixer, a grinder, a buffer. Any job that needed doing, the handy Home Motor could do. Marc Weiser, a scientist at Xerox, points out that the electric motor succeeded so well that it became invisible. Eighty years later nobody owns a Home Motor. We have instead dozens of micromotors everywhere. They are so small, so embedded, and so common that we are unconscious of their presence. We would have a hard time just listing all the motors whirring in our homes today (fans, clocks, water pumps, video players, watches, etc.). We know the industrial revolution succeeded because we can no longer see its soldiers, the motors.

Computer technology is undergoing the same disappearance. If the information revolution succeeds, the standalone desktop computer will eventually vanish. Its chips, its lines of connection, even its visual interfaces will submerge into our environment until we are no longer conscious of their presence (except when they fail). As the network age matures, we'll know that chips and glass fibers have succeeded only when we forget them. Since the measure of a technology's success is how invisible it becomes, the best long-term strategy is to develop products and services that can be ignored.

If it is not animated, animate it. Just as the technology of writing now covers almost everything we make (not just paper), so too the technologies of interaction will soon cover all that we make (not just computers). No artifact will escape the jelly bean chip; everything can be animated. Yet even before chips reach the penny price, objects can be integrated into a system *as if* they are animated. Imagine you had a million disposable chips. What would you do with them? It's a good bet that half of the value of those chips could be captured now, with existing technology, by creating a distributed swarmlike intelligence using such dumb power.

If it is not connected, connect it. As a first step, *every* employee of an institution should have intimate, easy, continuous access to the institution's medium of choice—email, voicemail, radio, whatever. The benefits of communication often don't kick in until ubiquity is approached; aim for ubiquity. Every step that promotes cheap, rampant, and universal connection is a step in the right direction.

Distribute knowledge. Use the minimal amount of data to keep all parts of a system aware of one another. If you operate a parts warehouse, for example, your system needs to be knowledgeable of each part's location every minute. That's done by barcoding everything. But it needs to go further. Those parts need to be aware of what the system knows. The location of parts in a warehouse should shift depending on how well they sell, what kind of backlog a vendor forecasts, how their substitutes are selling. The fastest-moving items (which will be a dynamic list) may want to be positioned for easier picking and shipping. The items move in response to the outside—if there is a system to spread the info.

Get machines to talk to one another directly. Information should flow laterally and not just into a center, but out and between as well. The question to ask is, "How much do our products/services know about our business?" How much current knowledge flows back into the edges? How well do we inform the perimeter, because the perimeter is the center of action.

If you are not in real time, you're dead. Swarms need real-time communication. Living systems don't have the luxury of waiting overnight to process an incoming signal. If they had to sleep on it, they could die in their sleep. With few exceptions, nature reacts in real time. With few exceptions, business must increasingly react in real time. High transaction costs once prohibited the instantaneous completion of thousands of tiny transactions; they were piled up instead and processed in cost-effective batches. But no longer. Why should a phone company get paid only once a month when you use the phone every day? Instead it will eventually bill for every call as the call happens, in real time. The flow of crackers off grocery shelves will be known by the cracker factory in real time. The weather in California will be instantly felt in the assembly lines of Ohio. Of course, not all information should flow everywhere; only the meaningful should be transmitted. But in the network economy only signals in real time (or close to it) are truly meaningful. Examine the speed of knowledge in your system. How can it be brought closer to real time? If this requires the cooperation of subcontractors, distant partners, and far-flung customers, so much the better.

Count on more being different. A handful of sand grains will never form an avalanche no matter how hard one tries to do it. Indeed one could study a single grain of sand for a hundred years and never conclude that sand can avalanche. To form avalanches you need millions of grains. In systems, more is different. A network with a million nodes acts significantly different from one with hundreds. The two networks are like separate species—a whale and an ant, or perhaps more accurately, a hive and an ant. Twenty million steel hammers swinging in unison is still 20 million steel hammers. But 20 million computers in a swarm is much, much more than 20 million individual computers.

Do what you can to make "more." In a network the chicken-and-egg problem can hinder growth at first—there's no audience because there is no content, and there is no content because there is no audience. Thus, the first efforts at connecting everything to everything sometimes yield thin fruit. At first, smart cards look no different from credit cards—just more inconvenient. But more is different; 20 million smart cards is a vastly different beast than 20 million credit cards.

It's the small things that change the most in value as they become "more." A tiny capsule that beeps and displays a number, multiplied by millions: the pager system. What if all the Gameboys or Playstations in the world could talk to one another? What if all the residential electric meters in a city were connected together into a large swarm? If all the outdoor thermometers were connected, we would have a picture of our climate a thousand times better than we have ever had before.

The ants have shown us that there is almost nothing so small in the world that it can't be made larger by embedding a bit of interaction in many copies of it, and then connecting them all together.

The game in the network economy will be to find the overlooked small and figure out the best way to have them embrace the swarm.

2 INCREASING RETURNS
Self-Reinforcing Success

Networks have their own logic. When you connect all to all, curious things happen.

Mathematics says the sum value of a network increases as the square of the number of members. In other words, as the number of nodes in a network increases arithmetically, the value of the network increases exponentially.* Adding a few more members can dramatically increase the value for all members.

This amazing boom is not hard to visualize. Take 4 acquaintances; there are 12 distinct one-to-one friendships among them. If we add a fifth friend to the group, the friendship network increases to 20 different relations; 6 friends makes 30 connections; 7 makes 42. As the number of members goes beyond 10, the total number of relationships among the friends escalates rapidly. When the number of people (n) involved is large, the total number of connections can be approximated as simply $n \times n$, or n^2. Thus a thousand members can have a million friendships.

The magic of n^2 is that when you annex one more new member, you

---

*I use the vernacular meaning of "exponential" to mean "explosive compounded growth." Technically, n^2 growth should be called polynomial, or even more precisely, a quadractic; a fixed exponent (2 in this case) is applied to a growing number n. True exponential growth in mathematics entails a fixed number (say 2) that has a growing exponent, n, as in 2^n. The curves of some polynomials and exponentials look similar, except the exponential is even steeper; in common discourse the two are lumped together.

add many more connections; you get more value than you add. That's not true in the industrial world. Say you owned a milk factory, and you had 10 customers who bought milk once a day. If you increased your customer base by 10% by adding one new customer, you could expect an increase in milk sales of 10%. That's linear. But say, instead, you owned a telephone network with 10 customers who talked to each other once a day. Your customers would make about n^2 (10^2), or 100 calls a day. If you added one more new customer, you increased your customer base by 10%, but you increased your calling revenue by a whopping 20% (since 11^2 is 20% larger than 10^2). In a network economy, small efforts can lead to large results.

A network's tendency to explode in value mathematically was first noticed by Bob Metcalfe, the inventor of a localized networking technology called Ethernet. During the late 1970s Metcalfe was selling a combination of Ethernet, Unix, and TCP/IP (the internet protocol), as a way to make large networks out of many small ones. Metcalfe says, "The idea that the value of a network equals n squared came to me after I failed to get networks to work on a small scale, despite many repeated experiments." He noticed that networks needed to achieve critical mass to make them worthwhile. But he also noticed that as he linked together small local networks here and there, the value of the combined large network would multiply abruptly. In 1980 he began formulating his law: value $= n \times n$.

In fact, n^2 underestimates the total value of network growth. As economic journalist John Browning notes, the power of a network multiplies even faster than this. Metcalfe's observation was based on the idea of a phone network. Each telephone call had one person at each end; therefore the total number of potential calls was the grand sum of all possible pairings of people with phones. But online networks, like personal networks in real life, provide opportunities for complicated three-way, four-way, or many-way connections. You can not only interact with your friend Charlie, but with Alice and Bob and Charlie at the same time. The experience of communicating simultaneously with Charlie's group in an online world is a distinct experience, separate in its essential qualities, from communicating with Charlie alone. Therefore, when we tally up the number of possible connections in a network we have to add up not only all the combinations in which members can be paired, but also all the possible groups as well. These additional combos send the total value of the network skyrocketing. The precise arithmetic is not important. It is enough to know that the worth of a network races ahead of its input.

This tendency of networks to drastically amplify small inputs leads to the second key axiom of network logic: the law of increasing returns. In one way or another this law undergirds much of the strange behavior in the network economy. The simplest version goes like this: The value of a network explodes as its membership increases, and then the value explosion sucks in yet more members, compounding the result.

An old saying puts it succinctly: Them that's got shall get.

A new way of saying it: Networks encourage the successful to be yet more successful. Economist Brian Arthur calls this effect "increasing returns." "Increasing returns" he says, "are the tendency for that which is ahead to get further ahead; for that which loses advantage to lose further advantage."

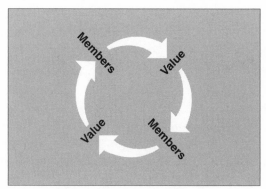

In networks, we find self-reinforcing virtuous circles. Each additional member increases the network's value, which in turn attracts more members, initiating a spiral of benefits.

In the industrial economy success was self-limiting; it obeyed the law of decreasing returns. In the network economy, success is self-reinforcing; it obeys the law of increasing returns.

We see the law of increasing returns operating in the way areas such as Silicon Valley grow; each successful new start-up attracts other start-ups, which in turn attract more capital and skills and yet more start-ups.

(Silicon Valley and other high-tech industrial regions are themselves tightly coupled networks of talent, resources, and opportunities.)

At first glance the law of increasing returns may seem identical to the familiar textbook notion of economies of scale: The more of a product you make, the more efficient the process becomes. Henry Ford leveraged his success in selling automobiles to devise more productive methods of manufacturing cars. This enabled Ford to sell his cars more cheaply, which created larger sales, which fueled more innovation and even better production methods, sending his company to the top.

That self-feeding circle is a positive feedback loop. While the law of increasing returns and the economies of scale both rely on positive feedback loops, there are two key differences.

First, industrial economies of scale increase value gradually and linearly. Small efforts yield small results; large efforts give large results. Networks, on the other hand, increase value exponentially—small efforts reinforce one another so that results can quickly snowball into an avalanche. It's the difference between a piggy bank and compounded interest.

Second, and more important, industrial economies of scale stem from the herculean efforts of a single organization to outpace the competition by creating value for less. The expertise (and advantage) developed by the leading company is its alone. By contrast, networked increasing returns are created and shared by the entire network. Many agents, users, and competitors together create the network's value. Although the gains of increasing returns may be reaped unequally by one organization, the value of the gains resides in the greater web of relationships.

These positive feedback loops are created by "network externalities." Anything that creates (or destroys) value which cannot be appointed to someone's account ledgers is an externality. The total value of a telephone system lies outside the total internal value of the telephone companies and their assets. It lies externally in the greater phone network itself. Networks are particularly potent sources of external value and have become a hot spot of economic investigation in the last decade. A parade of recently published academic papers scrutinize the fine points of network externalities: When do they arise? How do they break down? Are they symmetrical? Can they be manipulated?

One reason increasing returns and network externalities are garnering attention is because they tend to create apparent monopolies. Huge amounts of cash pour toward network winners such as Cisco or Oracle or Microsoft, and that makes everyone else nervous. Are network super-winners in fact monopolies? They are not like any monopolies of the industrial age. When antitrust hearings are conducted today, the witnesses are not customers angered by high pricing, haughty service, or lack of options—the traditional sins of a monopolist. Customers have nothing to complain about because they get lower prices, better service, and more features from network superwinners—at least in the short term. The only ones complaining about superwinners are their competitors, because increasing returns create a winner-take-most environment. But in the long term, the customer will have reason to complain if competitors pull back or disappear.

The new monopolies are different in several ways. Traditional monopolies dominated commodities. In the new order, as Santa Fe Institute economist Brian Arthur points out, "Dominance may consist not so much in cornering a single product as in successively taking over more and more threads of the web of technology." Superwinners can practice a type of crossover where control of one layer of the web leverages control into others. Owning the standard for voice phone calls can ease the likelihood of owning the standard for fax transmissions.

The unacceptable transgression of the traditional monopolist was that as a mono-seller (thus the Greek, mono-polist), it could push prices up and quality down. But the logic of the net inherently lowers prices and raises quality, even those of a single-seller monopolist. In the network economy, the unpardonable transgression is to stifle innovation, which is what happens when competition is stifled. In the new order, innovation is more important than price because price is a derivative of innovation.

Mono-sellers are actually desirable in a network economy. Because of increasing returns and n^2 value, a single large pool is superior to many smaller pools. The network economy will breed mono-sellers with great fertility. What is intolerable in a network economy is "monovation"—depending upon a single source of innovation. The danger of monopolists in the network economy is not that they can raise prices but they can become monovationists. But there are ways to encourage "polyvation"—

multiple sources of innovation—in a world of monopolists: by creating open systems, by moving key intellectual properties into the public domain, by releasing source code democratically. As we come to understand the importance of increasing returns and the other new rules of the network economy, we can expect shifts in our understanding of the role of market winners.

Industrial monopolies exploited simple economies of scale for their own benefit. Network effects are not about economies of scale, they are about value that is created above and beyond a single organization—by a larger network—and then returned to the parts, often unevenly. Because some portion of the value of a network firm so obviously comes from external sources, allegiance is often granted to external sources.

We see this in the way network effects govern the growth of Silicon Valley. Silicon Valley's success is external to any particular company's success, and so loyalty is external, too. As AnnaLee Saxenian, author of *Regional Advantage*, notes, Silicon Valley has in effect become one large, distributed company. People job-hop so frequently that folks "joke that you can change jobs without changing car pools. Some say they wake up thinking they work for Silicon Valley. Their loyalty is more to advancing technology or to the region than it is to any individual firm."

This trend seems likely to extend further. We are headed into an era when both workers and consumers will feel more loyalty to a network than to any ordinary firm. The great innovation of Silicon Valley is not the wowie-zowie hardware and software it has invented. Silicon Valley's greatest "product" is the social organization of its companies and, most important, the networked architecture of the region itself—the tangled web of former jobs, intimate colleagues, information leakage from one firm to the next, rapid company life cycles, and agile email culture. This social web, suffused into the warm hardware of jelly bean chips and copper neurons, creates a true network economy.

The social web, even in the Valley, displays some stress marks. There is no question that the network economy is, at worst, winner-take-all, and at best, winner-take-most. The trajectory of increasing returns and a shortage of attention focuses success toward a few points. Stars and hits rise, while the rest languish. Mundane appliances and bulky objects now seem to follow the Hollywood model: A few brands sell like crazy, and the rest sell only a few. It's a "hits" economy, where resources flow to those that show some life. If a new novel, new product, or new service begins to succeed it is fed more; if it falters, it's left to wither. Them that has, gets more.

The current great debate is whether the law of increasing returns favors the early or not. In some of the first studies of increasing returns, economist Brian Arthur discovered that when technological competitors, such as the VHS and Betamax video formats, were modeled in a computer, increasing returns favored one technology over the other—to the eventual demise of the unfortunate one (in this case Betamax). And "unfortunate" is the right word. According to Arthur's research, the technology that came to dominate, thanks to increasing returns, was not necessarily the superior one. It was just the lucky one. Or the early one. Arthur writes: "If a product or a company or a technology—one of many competing in a market—gets ahead by chance or clever strategy, increasing returns can magnify this advantage, and the product or company can go on to lock in the market."

All things being equal, early success has a measurable advantage. But in real life all things are rarely equal. Technologies which seem to be inferior and yet prevail through the dynamics of increased returns often reveal themselves under further study to be slightly superior in key ways. The Sony Betamax format lost to VHS because it couldn't record for as long as VHS could, and, according to some, because Sony discouraged Beta use for porno—an early use of video. Apple Computer's superior operating system lost to Windows because Apple had an inferior price—due to its misguided monopolist strategy. The supposedly ergonomic Dvorak keyboard lost to the all-too-familiar QWERTY keyboard because the Dvorak layout really wasn't any faster.

Being first or best sometimes helps, but not always. The outcome of competition in a network is not determined solely by the abilities of the competitors, but by tiny differences, including luck, that are greatly magnified by the power of positive feedback loops. The fate of competition is "path dependent" on minor nudges and hurdles that can "tip" the system in one direction or another. Final destiny cannot be predicted on the basis of exceptional attributes alone.

What can be predicted is the way in which networks enlarge small advantages, and then lock the advantage in. In the same way, initial parameters and conventions can quickly freeze into unalterable standards.

The solidifying standards of a network are both a blessing and a curse—a blessing because the ad hoc agreement reduces risk, and thus sparks widespread progress, and a curse because those who own or control the standard are disproportionately rewarded.

But the network economy doesn't allow the blessing without the curse. Microsoft's billions are tolerated (more or less) because so many others in the network economy have made their collective billions on the advantages of Microsoft's increasing-returns standards.

We forget how recent and sudden Microsoft's prominence is. Microsoft is a textbook example of Metcalfe's law ("The value of Windows increases exponentially as its users increase arithmetically") and the law of increasing returns ("The more who use NT, the more attractive NT becomes"). Microsoft also illustrates the third corollary of increasing returns: how small signals can suddenly become booms.

During its first 10 years, Microsoft's profits were negligible. Its profits rose above the background noise of Wall Street only around 1985. But once they began to rise, they exploded. A chart of Microsoft's cornucopia of profits is an exponentially booming curve, one that parallels several other rising stars in the network economy.

Federal Express experienced a similar trajectory: years of minuscule profit increases, slowly ramping up to an invisible threshold, and then surging skyward in a blast sometime during the early 1980s.

The story of fax machines is likewise a tale of a 20-year-long overnight success. After two decades of marginal success, the number of fax machines quietly crossed the point of no return during the mid-1980s—and the next thing you know, they were everywhere.

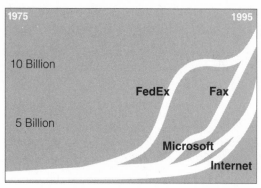

Network organizations experience small gains while their network is being seeded. Once the network is established, explosive growth follows with relatively little additional genius.

The archetypal case of a success explosion in a network economy is the Internet itself. As any proud old-time nethead will be happy to explain, the internet was a lonely (but thrilling!) cultural backwater for two decades before it showed up on the media radar. A graph of the number of internet hosts worldwide, starting in the 1970s, stays barely above the bottom line, until around 1991, when the global tally of hosts suddenly mushroomed, exponentially acting upward to take over the world.

The curves of Microsoft, the internet, fax machines and FedEx (I owe *Net Gain* author John Hagel credit for these four examples) are templates of exponential growth, compounding in a biological way. Such curves are almost the definition of a biological system. That's one reason the network economy is often described most accurately in biological terms. Indeed, if the web feels like a frontier, it's because for the first time in history we are witnessing biological growth in technological systems.

A good definition of a network is organic behavior in a technological matrix.

The compounded successes of Microsoft, FedEx, fax machines, and the internet all hinge on the prime law of networks: Value explodes exponentially with membership, and this heightened value acts like gravity drawing in yet more members. The virtuous circle inflates until all potential members are joined.

This explosion, however, did not ignite until approximately the late 1980s. Two things happened then—the dual big bangs of almost-free jelly bean chips and collapsing telco charges. It became feasible—that is, dirt cheap—to exchange data almost anywhere, anytime. The net, the grand net, began to precipitate out of this supersaturated solution. Network power followed.

One of the hallmarks of the industrial age was its reasonable expectations. Success was in proportion to effort. Small effort, small gains. Large effort, large gains. This linear ratio is typical of capital investments and resource allotments. According to data from the U.S. Statistical Abstract, the best-selling products in the 1950s—appliances such as refrigerators, clocks and washing machines—sold steadily with only a slight 2% annual increase in the number of units sold per year. To imagine the future of an enterprise or innovation one needed only to extrapolate the current trends in a straight line. There was a comfortable assumption—largely true—that the world proceeded linearly. Entirely new phenomenona did not ordinarily appear out of nowhere and change everything within months.

With the advent of large-scale electronic media networks in the mid century, that assumption began to erode. Millions of kids watching TV grew up to create rapid fads (hula hoops), instant youth cultures such as the beats and hippies, with sudden spontaneous gatherings of half a million, as at Woodstock. Events did not happen linearly. With media networks it was no longer safe to extrapolate the future from the recent past. When success came, it often fed on itself in crazy hyperkinetic booms. The recent sales of electronic pets is one example. Tamagotchis, the original brand of Japanese toy pets, went from sales of zero in Japan to 10 million units in their first year, to 20 million by the second year. When they were introduced in the United States a half million units were sold in the first month. The Tamagotchis could be actual breeding animals judging simply from their growth rate because their sales curve follows the population curve of reproducing biological animals. One day there are two pets, the next year there are 200. In biological populations, success can easily compound into runaway growth; now this wild runaway growth is happening with technology.

Everyday we see evidence of biological growth in technological systems. This is one of the marks of the network economy: that biology has taken root in technology. And this is one of the reasons why networks change everything.

Here's how this happened. Most of the technology in the early part of the century was relegated to the inside of a factory. Only businessmen cared about advancing technology—cheaper production methods or more specialized materials. The consumer products this advanced technology spun off into homes were, more often than not, labor-saving devices—sewing machines, vacuum cleaners, water pumps. They saved time, and thereby enhanced the prevailing culture. But the devices themselves (except for the automobile) were merely gadgets. They were *technology*—something foreign, best used in small doses, and clearly not the social and economic center of our lives. It was once very easy to ignore technology because it did not penetrate the areas of our lives we have always really cared about: our networks of friendship, writing, painting, cultural arts, relationships, self-identity, civil organizations, the nature of work, the acquisition of wealth, and power. But with the steady advent of technology into the networks of communication and transportation, technology has completely overwhelmed these social areas. Our social space has been invaded by the telegraph, the phonograph, the telephone, the photograph, the television, the airplane and car, then by the computer, and the internet, and now by the web.

Technology has become our culture, our culture technology.

Technology is no longer outside, no longer alien, no longer at the periphery. It is at the center of our lives. "Technology is the campfire around which we gather," says musician/artist Laurie Anderson. For many decades high tech was marginal in presence. Then suddenly—blink—it is everywhere and all-important.

Technology has been able to infiltrate into our lives to the degree it has because it has become more like us. It's become organic in structure. Because network technology behaves more like an organism than like a machine, biological metaphors are far more useful than mechanical ones in understanding how the network economy runs.

But if success follows a biological model, so does failure. A cautionary tale: One day, along the beach, tiny red algae suddenly blooms into a vast red tide. A few weeks later, just when the red mat seems indelible, it vanishes. Lemmings boom, then disappear as suddenly. The same biological forces that multiply populations can decimate them. The same forces that feed on one another to amplify network presences creating powerful standards overnight can also work in reverse to unravel them in a blink. The same forces that converge to build up organizations in so biological a fashion can also converge to tear them down. One can expect that when Microsoft's fortunes falter, their profits will plunge in a curve inversely symmetrical to their success. All the self-reinforcing reasons to join a network's success run in reverse when the success turns to failure and everyone wants to flee.

One more biological insight can be gleaned from the success of Microsoft, FedEx, and the internet. In retrospect one can see that at some point in their history the momentum toward them became so overwhelming that success became a runaway event. Success became infectious, so to speak, and spread pervasively to the extent that it became difficult for the uninfected to avoid succumbing. Take the arrival of the phone network. How long can you hold out not having a phone? Only 6% of U.S. homes are still holding out.

In epidemiology, the point at which a disease has infected enough hosts that it must be considered a raging epidemic can be thought of as the tipping point. The contagion's momentum has tipped from pushing uphill against all odds to rolling downhill with all odds behind it. In biology, the tipping points of fatal diseases are fairly high, but in technology, they seem to be triggered at much lower points.

There has always been a tipping point in any business, industrial or network, after which success feeds upon itself. However, the low fixed costs, insignificant marginal costs, and rapid distribution that we find in the network economy depresses tipping points below the levels of industrial times; it is as if the new bugs are more contagious—and more potent. It takes a smaller initial pool to lead to runaway dominance, sooner.

Lower tipping points also mean that the threshold of significance— the period before the tipping point during which a movement, growth, or innovation must be taken seriously—is also dramatically lower than it was during the industrial age. Detecting developments while they are beneath this threshold of significance is essential.

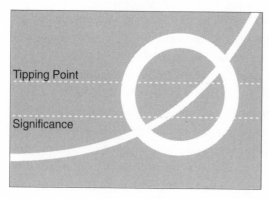

During the exponential gains peculiar to networks, compounding effects can pass a point of runaway growth. But it is before this point, before momentum builds, that one needs to pay attention.

Major U.S. retailers refused to pay attention to TV home-shopping networks during the 1980s because the number of people watching and buying from them was initially so small and marginalized that it did not meet the established level of retail significance. The largest U.S. retailers work in the realm of hundreds of millions. The first TV home shopping was dealing in the realm of thousands. Retailers discovered that shoppers would watch 50 hours of home-shopping programs before making their first purchase. The retailers considered this horrible news. But it turns out "watching others do it" was an initiation ritual. Shoppers trust other shoppers. Once shoppers were "invested" in the process by watching many others do it successfully, they kept coming back. So small numbers grew steadily and then rapidly as more shoppers brought in yet more shoppers. Instead of heeding the new subtle threshold of network economics, the retailers waited until the alarm of the tipping point sounded, which meant, by definition, that it was too late for them to cash in.

In the past, an innovation's momentum indicated significance. Now, in the network environment, where biological behavior reigns, significance precedes momentum.

One final parable rooted in biology. In a pond one summer a floating lily leaf doubles in size every day until it covers the entire surface of water. The day before it completely covers the pond, the water is only half covered, and the day before that, only a quarter covered, and the day before that, only a measly eighth. While the lily grows imperceptibly all summer long, only in the last week of the cycle would most bystanders notice its "sudden" appearance. By then, it is far past the tipping point.

The network economy is like a lily pond. Most of the pond looks empty, but a few lilies are doubling in size. The web, for example, is a leaf doubling every six months. Despite the one million web sites to date, the web's future has just begun. Other lily leaves are sprouting along the edges of the pond: MUDs, Irridium phones, wireless data ports, collaborative bots, WebTV, and remote solid state sensors. Right now, they are all just itsy-bitsy lily cells brewing at the beginning of a hot network summer. One by one, they will pass their tipping points, and suddenly become ubiquitous.

Strategies

Check for externalities. The initial stages of exponential growth looks as flat as any new growth. How can you detect significance before momentum? By determining whether embryonic growth is due to network effects rather than to the firm's direct efforts. Do increasing returns, open systems, n^2 members, multiple gateways to multiple networks play a part? Products or companies or technologies that get slightly ahead— even when they are second best—by exploiting the net's effects are prime candidates for exponential growth.

Coordinate smaller webs. The fastest way to amp up the worth of your own network is to bring smaller networks together with it so they can act as one larger network and gain the total n^2 value. The internet won this way. It was the network of networks, the stuff in between that glued highly diverse existing networks together. Can you take the auto parts supply network and coordinate it with the insurance adjusters network plus the garage repair network? Can you coordinate the intersection of hospital records with standard search engine technology? Do the networks of county property deed databases, U.S. patents, and small-town lawyers have anything useful in common? One thousand members in one network are far more powerful than one thousand members in three networks.

Create feedback loops. Networks sprout connections and connections sprout feedback loops. There are two elementary kinds of loops: Self-negating loops such as thermostats and toilet bowl valves, which create feedback loops that regulate themselves, and self-reinforcing loops, which are loops that foster runaway growth such as increasing returns and network effects. Thousands of complicated loops are possible using combinations of these two forces. When internet providers first started up, most charged users steeper fees to log on via high-speed modem; the providers feared speedier modems would mean fewer hours of billable online time. The higher fees formed a feedback loop that subsidized the provider's purchase of better modems, but discouraged users from buying them. But one provider charged less for high speed. This maverick created a loop that rewarded users to buy high-speed modems; they got more per hour and so stayed longer. Although it initially had to sink much more capital into its own modem purchases, the maverick created a huge network of high-speed freaks who not only bought their own deluxe modems but had few alternative places to go at high speed. The maverick provider prospered. As a new economy business concept, understanding feedback is as important as return-on-investment.

Protect long incubations. Because the network economy favors the nimble and quick, anything requiring patience and slowness is handicapped. Yet many projects, companies, and technologies grow best gradually, slowly accumulating complexity and richness. During their gestation period they will not be able to compete with the early birds, and later, because of the law of increasing returns, they may find it difficult to compete as well. Latecomers have to follow Drucker's Rule—they must be ten times better than what they hope to displace. Delayed participation often makes sense when the new offering can increase the ways to participate. A late entry into the digital camera field, for instance, which offered compatibility with cable TV as well as PCs, could make the wait worthwhile.

It's a hits game for everyone. In the network economy the winner-take-all behavior of Hollywood hit movies will become the norm for most products—even bulky manufactured items. Oil wells are financed this way now; a few big gushers pay for the many dry wells. You try a whole bunch of ideas with no foreknowledge of which ones will work. Your only certainty is that each idea will either soar or flop, with little in between. A few high-scoring hits have to pay for all the many flops. This lotterylike economic model is an anathema to industrialists, but that's how network economies work. There is much to learn from long-term survivors in existing hits-oriented business (such as music and books). They know you need to keep trying lots of things and that you don't try to predict the hits, because you can't.

Two economists proved that hits—at least in show biz—were unpredictable. They plotted sales of first-run movies between May 1985 and January 1986 and discovered that "the only reliable predictor of a film's box office was its performance the previous week. Nothing else seemed to matter—not the genre of the film, not its cast, not its budget." The higher it was last week, the more likely it will be high this week—

an increasing returns loop fed by word of mouth recommendations. The economists, Art De Vany and David Walls, claim these results mirror a heavy duty physics equation known as the Bose-Einstein distribution. The fact that the only variable that influenced the result was the result from the week before, means, they say, that "the film industry is a complex adaptive system poised between order and chaos." In other words, it follows the logic of the net: increasing returns and persistent disequilibrium.

3 PLENTITUDE, NOT SCARCITY
Value Flows from Abundance

Plentitude, not scarcity, governs the network economy. Duplication, replication, and copies run in excess. Whatever can be made, can be made in abundance. This plentitude:

- drives value
- works to open up closed systems
- spins off immense numbers of opportunities

Consider the first modern fax machine that rolled off the conveyor belt around 1965. Despite millions of dollars spent on its R&D, it was worth nothing. Zero. The second fax machine to be made immediately made the first one worth something. There was someone to fax to. Because fax machines are linked into a network, each additional fax machine that is shipped increases the value of all the fax machines operating before it.

This is called the fax effect. The fax effect dictates that plentitude generates value.

So strong is this power of plentitude that anyone purchasing a fax machine becomes an evangelist for the fax network. "Do you have a fax?" fax owners ask you. "You should get one." Why? Because your purchase increases the worth of their machine. And once you join the network, you'll begin to ask others, "Do you have a fax (or email, or Acrobat software, etc.)?" Each additional account you can persuade to join the network substantially increases the value of your account.

When you buy a fax machine, you are not merely buying a $200 box.

Your $200 purchases the entire network of all other fax machines in the world and the connections among them—a value far greater than the cost of all the separate machines. Indeed, the first fax machines cost several thousands of dollars and connected to only a few other machines, and thus were not worth much. Today $200 will buy you a fax network worth $3 billion.

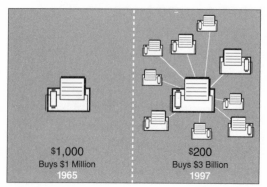

The low price of a fax machine today buys you an entire network, consisting of eighteen million machines. Each additional unit sold increases the value of your machine.

$1,000
Buys $1 Million
1965

$200
Buys $3 Billion
1997

In the network economy, the more plentiful things become, the more valuable they become.

This notion directly contradicts two of the most fundamental axioms we inherited from the industrial age.

First hoary axiom: Value comes from scarcity. Take the icons of wealth in the industrial age—diamonds, gold, oil, and college degrees. These were deemed precious because they were scarce.

Second hoary axiom: When things are made plentiful, they become devalued. For instance, carpets. They were once rare handmade items found only in houses of the rich. They ceased to be status symbols when they could be woven by the thousands on machines. The traditional law was fulfilled: commonness reduces value.

The logic of the network flips this industrial lesson upside down. In a network economy, value is derived from plentitude, just as a fax machine's value increases as fax machines become ubiquitous. Power comes from abundance. Copies are cheap. Let them proliferate.

Ever since Gutenberg made the first commodity—cheaply duplicated words—we have realized that intangible things can easily be copied. This lowers the value per copy. What becomes valuable is the relationships—sparked by the copies—that tangle up in the network itself. The relationships rocket upward in value as the parts increase in number even slightly.

Windows NT, fax machines, TCP/IP, GIF images, RealAudio—all born deep in the network economy—adhere to this logic. But so do metric wrenches, triple-A batteries, and other devices that rely on universal standards. The more common they are, the more it pays you to stick to that standard. We have an even older example in the English language. Wherever the expense of churning out another copy becomes trivial (and this is happening in more than software), the value of standards and the network booms.

In the future, cotton shirts, bottles of vitamins, chain saws, and the rest of the industrial objects in the world will also obey the law of plentitude as the cost of producing an additional copy of them falls steeply.

Proprietary, or "closed," systems were once rare because industrial systems were relatively uncomplicated. Proprietary systems rose in popularity as advancing technology made it difficult to replicate a system without assistance or encroaching on patents. The creators of a closed system made a nice living. When the information economy was first launched several decades ago, the dream was to own and operate a proprietary system—one that no one else could copy—and then let the money roll in. To a degree that can still be done, at least for short period, if the system is significantly superior. Bloomberg terminals in Wall Street traders' offices is one current example. But the network economy rewards the plentitude of open systems more than the scarcity of closed systems. It is a bit of a cliche now to blame Apple's misfortunes on its insistence that its operating systems be treated as a scarce resource but it's true. Apple had more than one opportunity to license its particularly wonderful interface—the now familiar desktop and windows design—but backed off each time, thereby guaranteeing its eventual eclipse by the relatively more open DOS and Windows systems.

There is a place for isolation in the infancy of systems, but openness is needed for growth because it taps into a larger wealth. Citibank pioneered the use of 24-hour instant cash at ATMs in the 1970s. They blanketed New York City with their proprietary machines, and at first this strategy was highly successful. Smaller competing banks started their own tiny and proprietary ATM networks, but they couldn't compete against the high penetration of Citibank machines. Then, led by Chemical Bank, these smaller banks banded together to form an open ATM network called Plus. The power of n^2 kicked in. Suddenly any ATM was your ATM. Citibank was invited to join the open Plus network but declined. Following the principle of increasing returns, the handy Plus system attracted more and more customers, and soon overwhelmed the once dominant Citibank. Eventually the open factor forced Citibank to forgo their proprietary ways and join.

Every time a closed system opens, it begins to interact more directly with other existing systems, and therefore acquires all the value of those systems.

In the mid 1980s I was associated with a pioneering online community called the Well. You dialed the Well's special modem, and once logged on you could chat, post, and email anyone you wanted—within the Well. All 2,000 members. Within a short time after start-up the Well made a big jump and opened its mail service to the then-obscure internet. The value of the Well suddenly skyrocketed in the view of its 2,000 or so members because now they could email thousands of academic professors or corporate nerds. A few years later, the Well further opened up its system to a capability called ftp, which allowed Well users to grab files on other internet servers and allowed others to grab files on the Well server. Again, the value of the Well exploded; with only a small effort it gained the tremendous value of the entire ftp network. Eventually the Well opened up even further, allowing users to join the conversation via the web, thereby acquiring all the value of the web.

There was a cost in each step. With every inclusion there was less control of the environment, more noise, more danger of disruption by accident or hacker, and more worry that the business model would collapse. At the same time it was obvious that a totally closed Well would have died.

The idea of plentitude is to create something that has as many systems and standards flowing through it as possible. The more networks a thing touches, the more valuable it becomes.

The value of an invention, company, or technology increases exponentially as the number of systems it participates with increases linearly.

The law of plentitude is not about dominance. The self-interest of ordinary business guarantees that every company in the world will strive to get its product or service into every home, or into every store. Popularity is an ancient goal. But that is not what network plentitude strives for.

The abundance upon which the network economy is built is one of opportunity.

While it is true that every additional email address in the world increases the value of all previous email addresses (that's the primary effect of plentitude) the increase in value happens because each email address is a node of opportunity, not just an artifact. An email address is more than a way to exchange memos. Because email is rooted in a network, opportunity runs in several directions at once. For instance, once it was realized that mail addresses could be archived easily (opportunity number one), it occurred to someone that they could be collected automatically (opportunity two). They could also be mailed to in bulk (opportunity three). The domain part of the address could be analyzed and used to detect patterns of usage (opportunity four). Addresses in a Rolodex could be updated automatically by the addressee (opportunity five). The address artifact itself could contain more than just a name; it could also hold other facets of interests that the owner was willing to exchange in certain circumstances (opportunity six).

A hammer is part of only a few networks, but a telephone is a part of many. The more networks a product or service can join, the more powerful it becomes.

Contrast this cascading abundance of opportunities with almost any product of the industrial age—say an electric rotary saw, or a color-fast dye, or a maplewood chair. While some of these objects have a few dual uses (the chair could be used as a step stool or to wedge a door open, and the saw motor could be used to drive a drill), they are pretty much limited to their designed intentions. There is no river of opportunities flowing from them. So that even if chairs, dye, and saws were to become universally abundant, their physical plentitude would not change the world much.

The power of the fax effect—more fax machines increasing the value of all previous machines—does not rely on the proliferation of Panasonic brand fax machines, or of any particular machine. Since many faxes are sent from laptop computers, or from a server somewhere, the power of plenty derives from opportunities rather than lumps of matter.

As opportunities proliferate, unintended uses take off. In the late 1970s, the Shah of Iran exiled his rival, the Ayatollah Khomeini, to Paris. Since the Shah controlled his country's media he assumed Khomeini would not be able to reach the Iranian people from France to stir up trouble. But sympathetic Iranian clergy exploited an unsuspected technological opportunity: the cassette tape. Every week in Paris Khomeini's friends recorded his inflammatory speeches on cheap recorders and smuggled copies (easily disguised as music tapes) into Iran, to be multiplied on $200 duplication machines and passed out to every mosque. On Fridays, Khomeini's sermons were played throughout Iran on boomboxes. The clerics turned the common tape deck into a broadcast network. I'm sure that not a single engineer who developed cassette tape technology ever envisioned it being used for broadcasting. Electronic media, because it is animated by electrons, is highly susceptible to being subverted by new uses.

Recently Sprint, the telecommunications company, pioneered flat cellular phone pricing—you could make all the cell phone calls you want for a fixed monthly fee. Within days of the pricing, the startled marketing experts at Sprint heard reports that people were using the cell phones as baby monitors. Parents would go into baby's bedroom with a cell phone, dial the kitchen, and then leave the line open. Voilà!

The more interconnected a technology is, the more opportunities it spawns for both use and misuse.

Some of the best video games of all time were elegant little programs that ran on early computers such as the Commodore 64. Millions of C-64s were sold during the early 1980s; most of them lie at the bottom of landfills today. Their flealike memories and lack of disk space have been replaced by Powerbooks and Pentiums. The few still working are sold at collector's prices. But out on the web, filling niches no one could have predicted, are a flock of emulators. You can download a Commodore 64 emulator onto your Powerbook. At the click of a button it will turn your state-of-the-art workstation into a moronic C-64 (or one of 25 other golden oldies) so you can play an ancient version of Moondust, or Pac-Man. This is equivalent to having a switch on the dashboard of your Ferrari to make it run like a VW Bug.

These refreshing street uses for technology stem from the plentitude of interactions. Artifacts of the industrial economy yield limited potential for such weird, tangential uses. The network economy, on the other hand, is a cornucopia of products and innovations that cry out to be subverted in new ways. Indeed, in a network, new opportunities arise primarily when existing opportunities are seized. A business that successfully occupies a niche immediately creates at least two new niches for other businesses. There is, for example, no end to the number of companies that will find a niche in email; the more wild ideas that are created, the more wild ideas can be created. The arms race between spammers and readers is only in its infancy.

The law of plentitude is most accurately rendered thus: In a network, the more opportunities that are taken, the faster new opportunities arise.

Furthermore, the number of new opportunities increases exponentially as existing opportunities are seized. Networks spew fecundity because by connecting everything to everything, they increase the number of potential relationships, and out of relationships come products, services, and intangibles.

A standalone object, no matter how well designed, has limited potential for new weirdness. A connected object, one that is a node in a network that interacts in some way with other nodes, can give birth to a hundred unique relationships that it never could do while unconnected. Out of this tangle of possible links come myriad new niches for innovations and interactions.

A network is a possibility factory.

So tremendous is the fount of plentitude in the network economy that having to deal with nearly infinite choices and mushrooming possibilities may be the limiting factor in the future. Navigating sanely through an expanding ocean of options is already difficult. The typical supermarket in America offers 30,000 to 40,000 products. The average shopper will zoom through the store in 21 minutes, and select out of those 40,000 choices about 18 items. This is an amazing feat of decision making. But it is nothing compared to what happens on the web. There are one million indexed web sites, containing 250 million pages. To be able to find the right page out of that universe is astounding, and the number of pages doubles every year. Dealing with this plentitude is critical because the totals of everything we manufacture in the world are only compounding. The total amount of information stored in the entire world—that's counting all the libraries, film vaults, and data archives—is estimated to be about 2,000 petabytes. (A petabyte is a billion megabytes, or about a quadrillion books the size of this one.) That's a lot of bits.

Plentitude will soon reach the level of zillionics. We know from mathematics that systems containing very, very large numbers of parts behave significantly different from systems with fewer than a million parts. Zillionics is the state of supreme abundance, of parts in the many millions. The network economy promises zillions of parts, zillions of artifacts, zillions of documents, zillions of bots, zillions of network nodes, zillions of connections, and zillions of combinations. Zillionics is a realm much more at home in biology—where there have been zillions of genes and organisms for a long time—than in our recent manufactured world. Living systems know how to handle zillionics. Our own methods of dealing with zillionic plentitude will mimic biology.

The network economy runs with plentitude. It vastly expands the

numbers of things, increases the numbers of intangibles with ease, multiplies the numbers of connections exponentially, and creates new opportunities without number.

Strategies

Touch as many nets as you can. Because the value of an action in
the network economy multiplies exponentially by the number of networks that action flows through, you want to touch as many other networks as you can reach. This is plentitude. You want to maximize the
number of relations flowing to and from you, or your service or product.
Imagine your creation as being born inert, like a door nail off a factory
conveyor belt. The job in the network economy is to link the nail to as
many other systems as possible. You want to adapt it to the contractor system by making it a standard contractor size so that it fits into standard air-
powered hammers. You want to give it a SKU designation so it can
be handled by the retail sales network. It may want a bar code so it can be
read by a laser-read checkout system. Eventually, you want it to incorporate a little bit of interacting silicon, so it can warn the door of breakage,
and take part in the smart house network. For every additional system the
nail is a part of, it gains in value. Best of all, the systems and all their
members also gain in value from every nail that joins.

And that's just for a stick of iron. More complex objects and services
are capable of permeating far more systems and networks, thus greatly
boosting their own value and the plentiful value of all the systems they
touch.

Maximize the opportunities of others. In every aspect of your business (and personal life) try to allow others to build their success around
your own success. If you run a hotel, what can you do to permit others—
airlines, luggage retailers, tour guides—to be part of your network?
Rather than viewing their dependency on your success as a form of para-
sitism, or worse, as a rip-off, understand this tight coupling as sustenance.
You want to entice others to create services centered around the customer attention you have won, or to supply add-ons to your product, or
even, if it is a new-fangled idea, to create legal imitations. This is a
counterintuitive stance at first, but it plays right into the logic of the net.

A small piece of an expanding pie is the biggest piece of all. Software is especially primed to work this way. The programmers who created the hit game *Doom* deliberately made it easy to modify. The results: Hundreds of other gamers issued versions of *Doom* that were vastly better than the original, but that ran on the *Doom* system. *Doom* boomed and so did some of the derivatives. The software economy is full of such examples. Third-party templates for spreadsheets, word processors, and browsers make profits for both the third-party vendor and the host system. It takes only a bit of imagination to see how the leveraging of opportunities also works in domains outside of software. When confronted with a fork in the road, if all things are equal, go down the path that makes the opportunities of others plentiful.

Don't pamper commodities; let them flow. The cost of replicating anything will continue to go down. As it does, the primary cost will be developing the first copy, and then getting attention to it. No longer will it be necessary to coddle most products. Instead they should be liberated to flow everywhere. Let's take pharmaceuticals, especially genetically bioengineered pharmaceuticals. The cost of little pills in the drug store can be hundreds of times greater than what they cost to produce in quantity, yet many drugs are priced expensively in order to recoup their astronomical development costs. Pharmaceutical companies treat and price their drugs as scarcities. One can expect, however, that in the future, as drug design becomes more networked, more data-driven, more computer mediated, and as drugs themselves become smarter, more adaptive, more animated, the competitive advantage will go to those companies that let "copies" of the drug flow in plentitude. For example, a highly evolved bioengineered headache relief drug may be sold for a few dollars on a "take as much as you need" basis. The company makes its profits when you pay it handsomely for tailoring that drug specifically for your DNA and your body. Once designed, you pay almost nothing for additional refills. Indeed there are already a few start-up biotech companies headed this way. The field is called pharmagenomics. They are heeding the call of plentitude.

Avoid proprietary systems. Sooner or later closed systems have to open up, or die. If an online service requires dialing a special phone number to reach it, it's moribund. If it needs a special gizmo to read it, it's kaput. If it can't share what it knows with competing goods, it's a loser.

Closed systems close off opportunities for others, making leverage points scarce. This is why the network economy—which is biased toward plenty—routes around closed systems. One could safely bet that America Online, WebTV, and Microsoft Network (MSN)—three somewhat closed systems—will eventually go entirely onto the open web, or disappear. The key issue in closed-versus-open isn't private versus public, or who owns a system; often private ownership can encourage innovation. The issue is whether it is easy or difficult for others to invent something that plays off your invention. The strategic question is simple: How easy is it for someone outside of the host company to contribute an advance to their system or product or service? Are the opportunities for participating in your own network scarce or plentiful?

Don't seek refuge in scarcity. Every era is marked by the wealth of those who figure out what the new scarcity is. There will certainly be scarcities in the network economy. But far greater wealth will be made by exploiting the plentitude. To make sure you are not seeking refuge in scarcity, ask yourself this question: Will your creation thrive if it becomes ubiquitous? If its value depends on only a few using it, you should reconsider it in light of the new rules.

4 FOLLOW THE FREE
Why the Net Rewards Generosity

The very best gets cheaper each year. This principle is so ingrained in our lifestyle that we bank on it without marveling at it. But marvel we should, because this paradox is a major engine of the new economy.

Before the industrial age, consumers could expect only slight improvements in quality for slight increases in price. Over the years the improved cost more. But with the arrival of automation and cheap energy in the industrial age, manufacturers could invert the equation: They offered lower costs and increased quality. Between 1906, when autos were first being made, and 1910, only four years later, the cost of the average car had dropped 24%, while its quality rose by 31%. By 1918, the average car was 53% cheaper than its 1906 counterpart, and 100% better in performance quality. The better-gets-cheaper magic had begun.

The arrival of the microprocessor accelerated this wizardry. In the information age, consumers quickly have come to count on drastically superior quality for drastically reduced price over time. A sensible recommendation to anyone asking for shopping advice today is that they should delay buying a consumer good until about 60 seconds before they actually need it. Indeed, a transportation specialist told me that almost nothing in the information industry is shipped by sea anymore; it all goes by air, so the price won't have a chance to drop while the product is in transit.

So certain is the plummet of prices that economists have mapped the curve of their fall. The cost of making something—whether it is steel, light bulbs, airplanes, flower pots, insurance policies, or bread—will drop over time as a function of the cumulative number of units produced. The more an industry makes, the better it learns how to make them, the more the cost drops. The downward price curve, propelled by organizational learning, is sometimes called the learning curve. Although it varies slightly in each industry, generally doubling the total output of something will reduce the unit cost on average by 20%.

Smart companies will anticipate this learning curve. Very smart companies will accelerate it by increasing volumes, one way or another. Since increasing returns can exponentially expand the demand of items—doubling their totals in months—network effects speed the steep fall of prices.

Computer chips further compound the learning curve. Better chips lower the cost of all manufactured goods, including new chips. Engineers use the virtues of computers to directly and indirectly create the next improved version of computers, quickening the rate at which chips are made, and their prices drop, which speed the rate at which all goods become cheaper. Around a circle the virtues go.

Feedback loops saturate networks. Since so many people and machines are interlinked in overlapping feedback loops, virtuous circles form. One, two, three, four, it all adds up to more.

- Expanding knowledge makes computers smarter.
- As computers get smarter we transfer some of that intelligence to the production line, lowering costs of goods and raising their perfection—including chips.
- Cheaper chips lower the cost of setting up a competing enterprise, so competition and spreading knowledge lowers the prices yet more.
- The know-how of cheapness spreads throughout industry quickly and makes its way back to the creation of better/cheaper chip and communication tools.

That virtuous circle feeds itself voraciously. So potent is compounding chip power that everything it touches—cars, clothes, food—falls under its spell. Prices dip and quality rises in all goods; not mildly, but precipitously. For example, between 1971 and 1989 a standard 17-cubic foot refrigerator declined in price by a third (in real dollars) while becoming

27% more energy efficient and sporting more features, such as ice-making. In 1988 Radio Shack listed a cellular phone for $1,500. Ten years later they list a better one for $200.

Most of the increase in value we've seen in products comes from the power of the chip. But in the network economy, shrinking chip meets exploding net to create wealth. Just as we leveraged compounded learning in creating the microprocessor revolution, we are leveraging the same amplifying loops in creating the global communications revolution. We can now harness the virtues of networked communications to directly and indirectly create better versions of networked communications. When quality feeds on itself in such a manner, we witness discontinuous change: in this case, a new economy.

Almost from their birth in 1971, microprocessors experienced steep inverted pricing. The chip's pricing plunge is called Moore's Law, after Gordon Moore, the Intel engineer who first observed the amazing, steady increase in computer power per dollar. Moore's Law states that computer chips are halving in price, or doubling in power every 18 months. Now, telecommunications is about to experience the kind of plunge that microprocessor chips have taken—but even more drastically. The net's curve is called Gilder's Law, for George Gilder, a radical technotheorist, who forecasts that for the foreseeable future (the next 10 years), the total bandwidth of communication systems will triple every 12 months.

The conjunction of escalating communication power with shrinking size of jelly bean nodes at collapsing prices leads Gilder to speak of bandwidth becoming free. What he means is that the price per bit transmitted drops down toward the free. What he does not mean is that telecom bills drop to zero. Telecom payments are likely to remain steady per month in real dollars as we consume more bits, just as those bits sink in cost.

The cost per bit sinks so low, however, that the per unit cost to the consumer closes in on the free. The cost follows what is called an asymptotic curve. In an asymptotic curve the price point forever nears zero without ever reaching it. It is like Zeno's tortoise: with each step forward, the tortoise gets halfway closer to the limit but never actually crosses it. The trajectory of an asymptotic curve is similar. It so closely parallels the bottom limit of free that it behaves as if it is free.

Because prices move inexorably toward the free, the best move in the network economy is to anticipate this cheapness.

So reliable is the arrival of cheapness in the new economy that a person can make a fortune anticipating it. One of the classic tales of counting on the cheap comes from the information era's Big Bang—when the semiconductor transistor was born.

In the early 1960s Robert Noyce and his partner Jerry Sanders—founders of Fairchild Semiconductor—were selling an early transistor, called the 1211, to the military. Each transistor cost Noyce $100 to make. Fairchild wanted to sell the transistor to RCA for use in their UHF tuner. At the time RCA was using fancy vacuum tubes, which cost only $1.05 each. Noyce and Sanders put their faith in the inverted pricing of the learning curve. They knew that as the volume of production increased, the cost of the transistor would go down, even a hundredfold. But to make their first commercial sale they need to get the price down immediately, with zero volume. So they boldly anticipated the cheap by cutting the price of the 1211 to $1.05, right from the start, before they knew how to do it. "We were going to make the chips in a factory we hadn't built, using a process we hadn't yet developed, but the bottom line: We were out there the next week quoting $1.05," Sanders later recalled. "We were selling into the future." And they succeeded. By anticipating the cheap, they made their goal of $1.05, took 90% of the UHF market share, and then within two years cut the price of the 1211 to 50 cents, and still made a profit.

In the network economy, chips and bandwidth are not the only things headed toward the asymptotic free. Calculation is too. The cost of computation—as measured by the millions of calculations per second per dollar—is headed toward the free. Transaction costs also dive toward the free. Information itself—headlines and stock quotes—plunges toward the free, too. Real-time stock quotes, for instance, were once high-priced insider information. Lately they have become so widely available that they must conform to a stock quote "spec" so that generic web browsers can read them uniformly.

Indeed, all items that can be copied, both tangible and intangible, adhere to the law of inverted pricing and become cheaper as they improve.

While it is true that automobiles will never be free, the cost per mile of driving will dip toward the free. It is the function (moving the body) per dollar that continues to drop. This distinction is important. Because while the function costs head toward zero, the expenditure share can remain steady, or even balloon. With cheaper costs we travel more, way more. With cheaper computation we consume billions of more calculations. Yet for vendors to make a profit, they must anticipate this cheapening per unit.

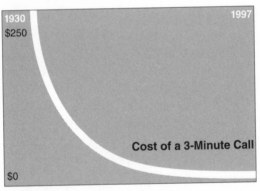

Gilder's Law says that the cost per communication bit will begin to sink farther than it has fallen previously. Eventually the cost of a telephone call, or of a bit transmitted, will be "free."

Let's take communications. All-you-can-use plain old telephone service with no frills will soon be essentially free. But as customers use more of this nearly free service, they quickly add options and deluxe services. First, every room gets a phone line. Then your car gets a line, or two. Then you get a mobile line. Then everyone in the family gets a mobile. Then answering service. Then call forwarding, call waiting, caller ID. Then fax and modem lines. Then all appliances and objects get a line. Then continuous open lines to cash registers, and credit card readers. Then security lines. Then ISDN and ADSL lines. Then caller ID blocking. Then junk call blocking. Then vanity phone numbers. Then portable personal numbers. Then voice mail sorting.

The outer boundaries of telephony keep expanding. When the phone was first invented, there was much confusion about what in the world it was good for commercially. Some thought it would be used to transmit music into homes. But even the most ambitious booster didn't envision having five phones lines in their home (as I do). The desire to have a phone in a car and to have caller ID was manufactured, indirectly, by the technology itself.

Technology *creates* an opportunity for a *demand*, and then fills it.

This is a very different notion of supply and demand from the one diagrammed in the introductory chapters of any economics textbook. The traditional supply and demand curve conveys a simple lesson: As a resource is consumed, it becomes more expensive to produce. For instance, as gold is mined, the easy (cheap) nuggets are found first; but to mine little particles of gold out of 25 tons of rock requires a higher gold price to make the effort worthwhile. Therefore, the supply curve slopes up, with the potential supply increasing as the price goes up. In contrast, the traditional understanding of demand says that demand slacks off the more supply there is. If you have lobster on Monday, Tuesday, and Wednesday, you'll be less interested in having it again and more inclined to pay less for lobster on Thursday. Therefore, the demand curve slopes down, with prices dropping as a product becomes abundant.

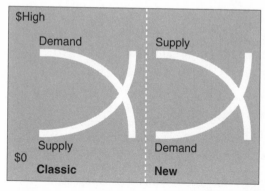

In textbook economics the supply of products would only increase if their price went up; in the new economics the supply increases as price goes down.

In the new order, as the law of plentitude kicks in and the nearly free take over, both of these curves are turned upside down. Paul Krugman, an economist at MIT, says that you can reduce the entire idea of the network economy down to the observation that "in the Network Economy, supply curves slope down instead of up and demand curves slope up instead of down." The more a resource is used, the more demand there is for it. A similar inversion happens on the supply side. Because of compounded learning, the more we create something, the easier it becomes to create more of it. The classic textbook graph is inverted.

As the supply curve rockets upward exponentially and the demand curve plunges further, the new Supply/Demand Flip suggests the two curves will cross each other at lower and lower price points. We see this already as the prices of goods and services keep heading toward the free. But hidden between the curves is a momentous surprise. Supply and demand are no longer driven by resource scarcity and human desire. Now both are driven by one, single exploding force: technology.

The accelerating expansion of knowledge and technology simultaneously pushes up the demand curve while pushing down the supply curve. One very potent force shifts both sides.

The effectiveness of technology in driving down prices is easy to appreciate. As stated at the beginning of this chapter, price drops have been going on for a while, although now it is accelerating. We know the outcome of this trend: lower prices everywhere. Consumers rejoice. But how are companies to make a profit in a world of constantly sinking prices? In the supply. Technology and knowledge are driving up demand faster than it is driving down prices. And demand, unlike prices, has no asymptote to limit it. The extent of human needs and desires is limited only by human imagination, which means, in practical terms, there is no limit.

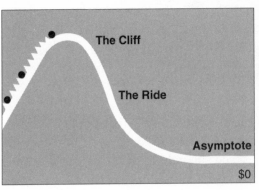

The Cliff

The Ride

Asymptote

$0

Anything that can be replicated will have a price that will tend toward zero, or free. While the cost may never reach free, it approaches the free in a curve called an asymptote.

The quicker the price of transportation drops, the more quality and services and innovation are embedded into cars, planes, and trains, lifting the quality of the "wants" they satisfy.

Over time, any product is on a one-way trip over the cliff of inverted pricing and down the curve toward the free. As the network economy catches up to all manufactured items—from cell phones to sofas—they will all slide down this slope of decreasing price more rapidly than ever.

The task, then, is to create new things to send down the slide—in short, to invent items and services faster than they are commoditized.

This is easier to do in a network-based economy because the crisscrossing of ideas, the hyperlinking of relationships, the agility of alliances, and the nimble quickness with which new nodes are created all support the constant generation of new goods and services.

We will create artifacts and services rapidly, as if they were short-lived bubbles. Since we can't hold back a bubble's drift toward popping, we can only learn to make more bubbles, faster.

If goods and services become more valuable as they become more plentiful, and if they become cheaper as they become valuable, then the natural extension of this logic says that the most valuable things of all should be those that are ubiquitous and free.

Ubiquity drives increasing returns in the network economy. The question becomes, What is the most cost-effective way to achieve ubiquity? And the answer is: give things away. Make them free.

Indeed, we see many innovative companies in the new economy following the free. Microsoft gives away its Internet Explorer web browser. Netscape also gives away its browser, as well as its valuable source code. Qualcomm, which produces Eudora, the popular email program, is given away as freeware in order to sell upgraded versions. Thomson, the $8 billion-a-year publisher, is giving away its precious high-priced financial data to investors on the web. Some one million copies of McAfee's antivirus software are distributed free each month. And, of course, Sun passed Java out gratis, sending its stock up and launching a mini-industry of Java application developers.

Can you imagine a young executive in the 1940s telling the board that his latest idea is to give away the first 40 million copies of his only product? (Fifty years later that's what Netscape did.) He would not have lasted a New York minute.

But now, giving away a product is a tested, level-headed strategy that banks on the network's new rules. Because compounding network knowledge inverts prices, the marginal cost of an additional copy (intangible or tangible) is near zero. It cost Netscape $30 million to ship the first copy of Navigator out the door, but it cost them only $1 to ship the second one. Yet because each additional copy of Navigator sold increases the value of all the previous copies, and because the more value the copies accrue, the more desirable they become, it makes a weird kind of economic sense to give them away at first. Once the product's worth and indispensability is established, the company sells auxiliary services or upgrades, continuing its generosity to involve more customers in a virtuous circle.

One might argue that this frightening dynamic works only with software, since the marginal cost of an additional copy is already near zero (now that software can be distributed online). But "following the free" is a universal law. Hardware, when networked, also follows this mandate. Cellular phones are given away in order to sell cell phone services. We can expect Direct-TV dishes to be given away for the same reasons. This principle applies to any object whose diminishing cost of replication is exceeded by the advantages of being plugged in.

As crackpot as it sounds, in the distant future nearly everything we make will (at least for a short while) be given away free—refrigerators, skis, laser projectors, clothes, you name it. This will only make sense when these items are pumped full of chips and network nodes, and thus capable of delivering network value.

The natural question is how companies are to survive in a world of such generosity? Three points will help.

First, think of "free" as a design goal for pricing. There is a drive toward the free—the asymptotic free—that, even if not reached, makes the system behave as if it has been reached. A very cheap rate can have an effect equivalent to being outright free.

Second, pricing a core product as free positions other services to be expensive. Thus, Sun gives Java away to help sell servers, and Netscape hands out consumer browsers to help sell commercial server software.

Third, and most important, following the free is a way to rehearse a service's or a good's eventual fall to free. You structure your business as if the thing that you are creating is free in anticipation of where its price is going. Thus, while Sega game consoles are not free to consumers, they are sold as loss leaders to accelerate their journey toward their eventual destiny—to be given away in a network economy.

Another way to view this effect is in terms of attention:

The only factor becoming scarce in a world of abundance is human attention.

As Nobel-winning economist Herbert Simon puts it: "What information consumes is rather obvious: It consumes the attention of its recipients. Hence a wealth of information creates a poverty of attention." Each human has an absolute limit of 24 hours per day to provide attention to the millions of innovations and opportunities thrown up by the economy. Giving stuff away captures human attention, or mind share, which then leads to market share.

Following the free also works in the other direction. If one way to increase product value is to make products free, then many things now free may contain potential value not yet perceived. We can anticipate the eruption of new wealth on the frontier by tracking down the free.

In the web's early days, the first indexes to this uncharted territory were written by students and given away. The indexes helped people focus their attention on a few sites out of the thousands available. Webmasters, hoping to draw attention to their sites, aided the indexers' efforts. Because they were free, indexes became ubiquitous. Their ubiquity quickly made them valuable (and their stockholders rich) and enabled many other web services to flourish.

What is free now that may later lead to extreme value? Where today is generosity preceding wealth? A short list of online candidates would be digesters, guides, catalogers, FAQs, remote live cameras, front page web splashes, and numerous bots. Free for now, each of these will someday have profitable companies built around them selling auxiliary services. Digesting, guiding and cataloging are not fringe functions, either. In the industrial age, a digest, *Reader's Digest*, was the world's most widely read magazine; a guide, *TV Guide*, was more profitable than the three major networks it guided viewers to; and a catalog of answers, the *Encyclopaedia Britannica*, began as a compendium of articles written by amateurs—something like online FAQs (Frequently Asked Questions).

But the migration from ad hoc use to commercialization cannot be rushed. To reach ubiquity you need to pass through sharing.

Increasingly we see technologies pass through a protocommercial stage. Huge numbers of people, exerting millions of hours of collective effort, will jointly craft hundreds of thousands of creations, but without the exchange of money. An entire society following the free! Author Lewis Hyde long ago called this arrangement a gift economy. The central task in a gift economy is to keep the gifts moving. By social debt, barter, and pure charity, gifts circulate and generate happiness and wealth.

The early internet and the early web sported amazingly robust gift economies. Text and expertise (FAQs, for example) and services (page designs) were swapped, shared generously, or donated outright. Information was bartered, content was given away, code was exchanged. For a long while the gift economy was the only way to acquire things online. In the first 1,000 days of the web's life, several hundred thousand webmasters created over 450,000 web sites, thousands of virtual communities, and 150 million pages of intellectual property, primarily for free. And these protocommercial sites were visited by 30 million people around the world, with 50% of them visiting daily, staying for an average of 10 minutes per day. This is a raging success by almost any measure you'd want to use. No other emerging media in the past experienced such glory so early in its growth.

Talk of generosity, of information that wants to be free, and of virtual communities is often dismissed by businesspeople as youthful new age idealism. It may be idealistic but it is also the only sane way to launch a commercial economy in the emerging space. "The web's lack of an obvious business model right now is actually its main event," says Stewart Brand, of the Global Business Network.

When a sector of the new economy passes through the protocommercial phase, it is the opposite of the "tragedy of the commons." The tragedy of the commons was that nobody took responsibility for maintaining the communal pastures that were the livelihood for the entire community. In the follow-the-free economy that seems to precede commercial activity on the net, *everyone* keeps the commons up because nobody is able to make a living from it on their own. Sophisticated software, as good as anything you can purchase, is written, debugged, supported, and revised for free in this "triumph of the commons."

The most popular software used to run web sites is called Apache. It is not sold by Netscape, or Microsoft, or anyone. Apache, which has 47% of the server market (Microsoft has 22% and Netscape 10%), was written (and is maintained) by a network of volunteers. It is given away free. Apache, which is used by the developers of such commercial sites as McDonald's, keeps getting better because the triumph of the commons rewards a completely open product: Anyone has access to Apache's software source code and can improve it. "If you give everyone source code, everyone becomes your engineer," says John Gage, chief scientist at Sun Microsystems.

The most popular operating system for web server workstations is not sold by anyone. It is a product called Linux, a Unix-compatible program that was originally written by Linus Torvalds, and given away for free. In the manner of building medieval cathedrals, hundreds of software engineers volunteer their time and expertise to refine and improve Linux, and to keep it free. Beside Apache and Linux, there are many other free software suites, such as Perl and X-Windows, maintained by a network of programmers. The engineers don't get paid in money; rather they get better tools than they can buy, tools that can be easily tweaked by them for maximum performance, tools superior to what they can make alone, and tools that increase in network value, since they are given away.

Tens of thousands of software programs written for almost every imaginable use are available on the net for free. Called shareware, the model is simple. Download whatever software you want for free, try it out, and if you like it, send some money to the author. Dozens of entrepreneurs have made their million dollars selling goods by this protocommercial method. More and more, the triumph of the commons overrides orthodox business models.

As Stewart Brand says, the *main event* of the emerging World Wide Web is its current absence of a business model in the midst of astounding abundance. The gift economy is one way players in the net rehearse for a life of following the free and anticipating the cheap. This is also a way for entirely new business models to shake out. Furthermore the proto-commercial stage is a way for innovation to fast-forward into hyperdrive. Temporarily unhinged from the constraints of having to make a profit by next quarter, the greater network can explore a universe of never-before-tried ideas. Some ideas will even survive the transplantation to a working business.

It's a rare (and foolish) software outfit these days that does not intro-duce its wares into the free economy as a beta version in some fashion. Fifty years ago the notion of releasing a product unfinished—with the in-tention that the users would help complete it—would have been consid-ered either cowardly, cheap, or inept. But in the new regime, this precommercial stage is brave, prudent, and vital.

Releasing incomplete "buggy" products is not cost-cutting des-peration; it is the shrewdest way to complete a product when your customers are smarter than you are.

The protocommercial state and the triumph of the commons is in as-cendance. It is no coincidence that increasing numbers of internet com-panies take themselves public before they are profitable. Investors are purchasing shares in a firm with protocommercial value. The old guard reads this as a signal of greed, speculation, and hype. But it also signals that many of the components of the gift economy—attention, commu-nity, standards, and shared intelligence—have to be in place before cold-cash commercialization can kick in. The gift economy is a rehearsal for the radical dynamics of the network economy.

Strategies

What can you give away? This is the most powerful question in this book. You can approach this question in two ways: What is the closest you can come to making something free, without actually pricing it at zero? Or, in a true gesture of enlightened generosity, you can figure out how to part with something very valuable for no monetary return at all. If either strategy is pursued with intelligence, the result will be the same.

The network will magnify the value of the gift. But giving something away is not usually easy. It must be the right gift, given in the proper context. To figure out what to give away, consider these questions:

- Is the freebie more than a silly premium, like the toy in a cereal box? There is no power in the gift unless it is crucial to your business.
- What virtuous circle will this freebie circulate in? Is it the loop you most need to amplify?
- In the long run, the unbounded support of a customer is more valuable than a fixed amount of their money. How will you eventually capture the support of customers if there is initially no flow of money?

Every organization harbors at least one creation—or potential creation—that can be liberated into "free-dom." This is often an idea with problems, particularly with its price: Should it be $69.50 per minute or $6.50 per box? The answer sometimes is: It should be free. Even if the idea is never actualized, my experience is that the very act of contemplating the free will inevitably illuminate all kinds of beneficial attributes that were never visible before. "Free" has long been a taboo price point. Perhaps because it has been forbidden, many low-hanging fruit are waiting to be plucked by giving the free serious consideration.

Act *as if* your product or service is free. Magazine publishers do this. The cover price on a magazine barely covers the cost of printing it, so publishers act as if they were giving it away (and some actually do). They make their money instead on advertising. Says pundit Esther Dyson, "The creator who immediately writes off the costs of developing content—as if it were valueless—is always going to win over the creator who can't figure out how to cover those costs." Memberships in serious discounters such as Cendant are also "as if free." Cendant "gives away" the merchandise very near the cost of manufacturing, as if the stuff were free. They make the bulk of their profits not from selling goods to its members—who get fantastic retail prices—but from selling $40 per year membership fees.

Invest in the first copy. That is the only one that will hurt. The second copy and all thereafter will head toward the free, but the first will become increasingly more expensive and capital intensive. Gordon Moore, of Moore's Law fame, posed a second law: that the costs of inventing chips (that are halving in cost every 18 months) is doubling every three to four years. The up-front investment for research, design, and process invention for all complex endeavors are commanding a larger share of the budget, while the capital costs of subsequent copies diminishes.

Anticipate the cheap. What would you do if your current offerings cost only one third what they cost today? They *will* someday soon, so create models that recognize this trend.

Turn off the meter, charge for joining. Flat or monthly fixed pricing is one way of pricing "as if free." Fees are paid, but there is no meter running. This tactic can be abused by the company (a la cable TV) or can be abused by the consumer (a la AOL). A flat fee is one type of subscription. Subscriptions are well-honed tools used by the soft world of magazines and theater, among others. Could subscriptions really apply to old order physical products, like say, food? The idea of subscribing to food is not so outlandish. Forty years ago subscriptions to milk were quite common. There were also subscriptions to bread and beer and other staples. Subscriptions tend to emphasize and charge for intangible values: regularity, reliability, first to be served, and authenticity, and work well in the arena of "as if free."

The ancillary market is the market. The software is free, but the manual is $10,000. That's no joke. Cygnus Solutions, based in Sunnyvale, California, rakes in $20 million per year in revenues selling support for free Unix-like software. Apache is free but you can buy support and upgrades from C2Net. Although Novell, the network provider, does sell network software, that's not what they are really selling, says Esther Dyson: "What Novell Inc. really is selling is its certified NetWare engineers, instructors, and administrators, and the next release of NetWare." One educational software exec admitted that his company's help line was actually an important profit center. Their main market was the ancillary products they sold for their flagship software, which they had a chance to do while helping customers.

Pinpoint where value is being given out for free now, and then follow up. The next Netscape, the next Yahoo, the next Microsoft is already up and running, and they are giving their stuff away for free. Find them, and hitch your wagon to their star. Look for the following tricks: charges only for ancillaries, as-if-free behavior, memberships, and outright generosity. If they are using the free to play off network effects, they are the real McCoys.

5 FEED THE WEB FIRST
Members Prosper as the Net Prospers

The distinguishing characteristic of networks is that they contain no clear center and no clear outside boundaries. Within a network everything is potentially equidistant from everything else.

Therefore the first thing the network economy reforms is our identity.

The vital distinction between the self (us) and the nonself (them)—once exemplified by the fierce loyalty of the organization man in the industrial era—becomes less meaningful in a network economy. The only "inside" now is whether you are on the network or off.

Individual allegiance moves away from firms and toward networks and network platforms.

Are you Windows or are you Mac?
This shift to network loyalty makes the potential of any network we might want to join a key issue. Is the network waxing or waning? Is the upside potential meager or tremendous? Is the network open or closed?
When given the choice between closed or open systems, consumers show a fierce enthusiasm for open architectures. They choose the open again and again because an open system has more potential upside than a closed one. There are more sources from which to recruit members and more nodes with which to intersect.
Identifying the preferred network to do business in is now a major

chore for firms. Because more and more of a firm's future lies in its networks, firms must evaluate a network's relative open- and closedness, its circulation, its ability to adapt. Consultant John Hagel says, "A web limits risk. It allows companies to make irreversible investments in the face of technological uncertainty. Companies in a web enjoy expanding sourcing and distribution options, while their fixed investment and skill requirements fall."

As the destiny of firm and web intertwine, the health of the matrix becomes paramount.

Maximizing the value of the net itself soon becomes the number one strategy for a firm. For instance, game companies will devote as much energy to promoting the platform—the tangle of users, game developers, and hardware manufacturers—as they do to their games. For unless their web thrives, they die. This represents a momentous change—a complete shift in orientation. Formerly, employees of a firm focused their attention on two loci: the firm itself and the marketplace.

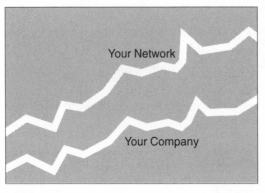

The prosperity of a firm is directly linked to the prosperity of its network. As the platform or standard it operates on flourishes, so does the firm.

Now there is a third horizon to consider: the network. The network consists of subcontractors, vendors and competitors, emerging standards for exchanges, the technical infrastructure of commerce, and the web of consumers and clients.

Commerce networks can be thought of as ecologies. Economist Brian Arthur states: "Players compete not by locking in a product on their own but by building webs—loose alliances of companies organized around a mini-ecology—that amplify positive feedbacks to the base technology."

During certain phases of growth, feeding the network is as important as feeding the firm. Some firms that already have large market shares (such as Intel, which owns 80% of the PC processor market) channel money, through minority investments, to younger firms whose success will strengthen the market for their products, directly or indirectly. They feed the web because it is good business.

In the network economy a firm's primary focus shifts from maximizing the firm's value to maximizing the network's value.

Not every network demands the same investment. The music CD standard and web of suppliers is well entrenched by now. The new DVD video standard is not. A publishing company issuing music on a CD has to devote less energy to making sure the CD platform flourishes than does a movie company issuing their film on a DVD. The film company must devote substantial resources to ensuring the spread and survival of this emerging platform. They'll work with the hardware manufacturers, maybe share costs of advertising by seeding the platform logo in their own ads, send reps to technical committees, and cooperate with other film studios in getting the new format accepted. The music company doesn't need to make as heavy an investment with CDs. But they do need to make investments into new networks if they try to deliver music online—because online delivery is still in its embryonic phase.

Every network technology follows a natural life cycle, roughly broken into three stages:

- Prestandard
- Fluid
- Embedded

A firm's strategy will depend on what phase a network is in.

The prestandard phase is the most exciting. This period is marked by tremendous innovation, high hopes, and grand ambition. "Aha!" ideas flow readily. Since there are no experts, everyone can compete, and it seems as if everyone does. Easy entry into the field draws myriad players.

For instance, when telephone networks began, there were few standards and many contenders. In 1899, there were 2,000 local telephone firms in the American telephone network, many of them running with their own standards of transmission. In a similar vein, in the 1890s, electricity came in a variety of voltages and frequencies. Each local power plant chose one of many competing standards for electrical power. Transportation networks, ditto. As late in the railroad era as 1880, thousands of railway companies did not share a universal gauge.

Two examples of networks in the prestandard stage today are online video and e-money. You have the choice of many competing protocols with equal prospects. With both domains, the uncertainty level is high, but the consequences of being wrong are minimal. Little is locked in, so it's easy to change.

Networks in the fluid phase have a different dynamic. The plethora of choices in the prestandard phase gradually reduces to two or three. Allegiances are mobile, and drift over time. During this period, networks demand the strongest commitment to their survival. Participants have to feed the web of their choice first, and the narrowing of choices allows substantial investment to spur rapid growth. The effects of plentitude and increasing returns kick in—more breeds more. Feeding the web on any of several standards still produces gains for all participants. Yet it is inevitable that only one standard will ultimately prevail while the other ones fail. The uncertainty level is nearly as high as during the prestandard phase, but the risks for being wrong are greater. Anyone who remembers the demise of 8-track audiotapes will appreciate the perils of this painful stage. Today such networks as digital photographs and desktop operating systems are in this fluid phase: Several well-established standards vie for ultimate dominance. Choose wisely!

The final stage in the life cycle of networks is the embedded phase, where one standard is so widely accepted that it becomes embedded in the fabric of the technology and is thereafter nearly impossible to dislodge—at least as long as the network exists. Regular 110-volt AC power is well embedded at this point (although, as the power grid becomes global, there could be some surprises). ASCII text is likewise deeply embedded—at least for phonetic languages. Some of the conventions of voice dial tone are so ubiquitous worldwide as to be permanent.

In any phase of innovation—prestandard, fluid, or embedded—

standards are valuable because they hasten innovation. Agreements are constraints on uncertainty. The constraints of a standard solidify one pathway out of many, allowing further innovation and evolution to accelerate along that stable route. So central is the need to cultivate certainty that organizations must make the common standard their first allegiance. As standards are established, growth takes off.

For maximum prosperity, feed the web first.

Arriving at standards is often easier said than done. Standard-making is a torturous, bickering process every time. And the end result is universally condemned — since it is the child of compromise. But for a standard to be effective, its adoption must be voluntary. There must be room to dissent by pursuing alternative standards at any time.

Standards play an increasingly vital role in the new economy. In the industrial age, relatively few products demanded standards. You didn't need a consensual network to make a chair and table. If you obeyed some basic ergonomic conventions — make table height 30 inches — you were on your way. Those industrial products that operated in networks — such as the electrical or transportation networks — demanded sophisticated standard-making. Anything plugged into the electrical grid had to be standard. Automobiles manufactured by separate factories shared standards on such things as axle width, fuel mixtures, placement of turn signals, not to mention the many standards of road construction and signage.

All information and communication products and services demand extensive consensus. Participants at both ends of any conversation have to understand each other's language. Multiply one conversation by a billion, factor in a thousand different media choices, and then start to count three-way, four-way, n-way conversations, and the amount of consensus-setting skyrockets.

In the network economy, ever-less energy is needed to complete a single transaction, but ever-more effort is needed to agree on what pattern the transaction should follow.

Thus "feeding the web first" increases in necessity. Businesses can expect to devote great intellectual capital on formulating, negotiating, deciding, forecasting, and adhering to emerging standards. The question "Which platform do we back?" will not be confined to PCs. It will be asked in regard to calendars, cars, accounting principles, and even currencies.

As more of the economy migrates to intangibles, more of the economy will require standards.

But consumers will groan under the load of decisions. There is a ying-yang tradeoff in the new economy. The ying, or positive side, is that consumers keep most of the gains in productivity that are earned by technology. Competition is so severe, and transactions so "friction-free," that most of each cycle's betterment goes not to corporate profits but to consumers in the form of cheaper prices and higher quality.

The yang, or downside, is that consumers have a never-ending onslaught of decisions to make about what to buy, what standard to join, when to upgrade or switch, and whether backward compatibility is more important than superior performance. The fatigue of sorting out options and allegiances, or recovering from them, is underappreciated at the moment, but will mount. The joy of the new economy is that the next version is almost free; the bane is that no one wants the hassle of upgrading to it, even if you pay them to do it.

The fatigue will only worsen. The net is a possibility factory, churning out novel opportunities by the screenful. Unharnessed, this explosion can drown the unprepared. Standardizing choices helps tame the debilitating abundance of competing possibilities. This is why the most popular sites on the web today are meta-sites that sort the abundance and point you to the best.

Since the network economy is so new, we as a society have paid little attention to how standards are created and how they grow. But we should notice, because once implemented, a successful standard tends to remain forever. And standards themselves shape behavior.

I was associated with the genesis of the Well, one of the first public computer conferencing systems to be plugged into the internet. The Well was conceived and built by others, but as director of the poor non-profit that owned it, and as one of the first participants to join when it opened, I was involved in creating its policies. It became clear almost from day one that the technical specifications of the software that the Well used directly shaped the kind of community growing within it. Other models of conferencing software used elsewhere produced different kinds of communities. The Well's software—as implemented by the Well—encouraged linear conversations and community memory; it discouraged anonymity, but encouraged responsibility for words and topics; it permitted limited forms of dissent and retraction, and it allowed users to invent their own tools. It did all this primarily by means of Unix code—by the software standards set up within the Well—rather than by posted rules. The community it shaped was distinctive and long-lived. In fact the community, with all its quirks, is still going, even though the software that runs it has evolved into a web browser interface. The behavior-changing standards remain. The power to mold a community by code rather than regulation was eventually articulated by Well users into a serviceable maxim: Peace through tools, not rules.

The internet and the web also contain toolish standards that invisibly shape our behavior. We have ideas about ownership, about accessibility, about privacy, and about identity that are all shaped by the code of HTML and TCP/IP, among others. Currently only a small portion of our lives flow through these webs, but as cyberspace subsumes televisionspace and phonespace and much of retailspace, the influence of standards upon social behavior will grow.

Eventually technical standards will become as important as laws.

Laws are codified social standards; but in the future, codified technical standards will be just as important as laws. Harvard Law professor Lawrence Lessig says, "Law is becoming irrelevant. The real locus of regulation is going to be (computer) code." As networks mature, and make the transition from ad hoc prestandard free-for-alls to fluid hot spots of innovation, and then into full-fledged systems with deeply embedded standards, standards increasingly ossify into something like laws.

Standards also harden with age. They become resistant to change and they descend into *hard*ware. Their code gets wired into the backs of chips, and as the chips spread, the standard infiltrates ever more deeply.

An elaborate process of legal overview monitors and analyzes our lawmaking. So far we have little of the sort for our standard-making, although these agencies, such as the ITU (International Telecom Union) will soon be as influential as courts. Standards are not just about technology. They are about soft and fuzzy things such as options and relationships and trust. They are social instruments. They create social territory.

A network is like a country in that it is a web of relationships regulated by standards. In a country citizens pay taxes and adhere to laws for the benefit of all. In a network, netizens feed the web first for the benefit of all. The network economy is a meta-country. Its web of relationships differ from those of a country in three ways:

- No geographical or temporal boundaries exist—relations flow ceaselessly 24 by 7 by 365.
- Relations in the network economy are more tightly coupled, more intense, more persistent, more diverse, and more intimate in many ways than most of those in a country.
- Multiple overlapping networks exist, with multiple overlapping allegiances.

These hyperconnections can either strengthen or weaken traditional relationships. The extremely personal, highly trust-bound relations in a family stand to be strengthened, while the diffuse and nearly contractual relations in a nation-state are liable to weaken. Yet, as Peter Drucker points out, "The nation-stare is not going to wither away. It may remain the most powerful political organ around for a long time to come, but it will no longer be the indispensable one." In its stead we'll rely on nongovernmental agencies such as the Red Cross, ACLU, HMOs, insurance giants, the net and the web, and UN-like entities. These parapolitical organizations will supplement the embedded nation-state. They will be the indispensable networks we care about.

In both country and network, the surest route to raising one's own prosperity is raising the system's prosperity. The one clear effect of the industrial age is that the prosperity individuals achieve is more closely related to their nation's prosperity than to their own efforts. Lester Thurow, an MIT economist, has pointed out that enabling the lowest paid to earn more is the best way to raise wages for the highest paid—the theory being that a rising tide lifts all boats. The network economy will only amplify this.

To raise your product, lift the networks it ties into. To raise your company, lift the standards it supports. To raise your country, increase the connections (in quality and quantity) that allow others to prosper.

To prosper, feed the web first.

The web is underfed right now. It is small compared to the rest of the world. In 1998 the internet boasted of an estimated 120 million people with access. But that means only 2% of human adults have a direct line to the online network.

But the net is growing exponentially fast. If current rates continue, by early in the new century, 1 billion people will have internet access, 75% of adults will access to some kind of phone, and, according to Nicholas Negroponte, there will 10 billion electronic objects connected together online. Every year the net engulfs more of the world.

The net is moving irreversibly to include everything of the world.

As the net takes over, many observers have noted the gradual displacement in our economy of materials by information. Automobiles weigh less than they once did and yet perform better. Industrial materials have been replaced by nearly weightless high-tech know-how in the form of plastics and composite fiber materials. Stationary objects are gaining information and losing mass, too. Because of improved materials, high-tech construction methods, and smarter office equipment, new buildings today weigh less than comparable ones from the 1950s. So it

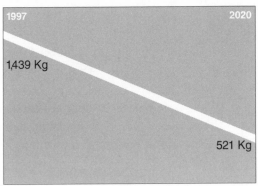

1997   2020

1,439 Kg

521 Kg

Even industrial objects like automobiles follow new rules. An automobile's average weight is dropping and will continue to drop as information replaces its mass.

isn't only your radio that is shrinking, the entire economy is losing weight too.

Even when mass is conserved, information increases. An average piece of steel manufactured in 1998 was vastly different from an average piece of steel made in 1950. Both pieces weighed approximately the same, but the one made recently is far superior in performance because of the amount of design, research, and knowledge that went into its creation. Its superior value is not due to extra atoms, but to extra information.

The wholesale migration from mass to bits began with the arrival of computer chips. This subtle disembodiment was first viewed as a unique dynamic of the high-tech corridors of Silicon Valley. Software was so strange—part body, part spirit—that nobody was surprised when the computer industry itself behaved strangely. The principles of the net, such as increasing returns, were seen as special cases, anomalies within the larger "real" economy of steel, oil, automobiles, and farms. What did such weirdness have to do with, say, making cars, or selling lettuce? At first, nothing. But by now every industry (shoe retail, glass manufacturing, hamburgers) has an information component, and that component is increasing. There is not a single company of consequence that does not use computers and communication technology. All U.S. companies (low as well as high-tech) together spent $212 billion on information technology in 1996. Often, the digital component of the firm, say the IT or MIS department, or the wizards running the technology, will be the first to feel the influence of the new rules and network dynamics. Consultants Larry Downes and Chunka Mui say, "Even though the primary technology of many industries may not be in transition . . . *every* industry is going through a revolution in its information technology." As more of a company "goes online" nerd ideas begin to seep into the whole organization, reshaping the firm's understanding of what it is doing. Over time, more and more employees will chase the opportunities that intensive information and communication networks bring.

New network technology and globalization accelerates the disembodiment of goods and services. The new dynamics of information will gradually supersede the old dynamics of industrialization until network behavior becomes the entire economy.

Bit by bit, the logic of the network will overtake every atom we deal with.

The logic of the network will spread from its base in silicon chips, to infiltrate steel, plywood, chemical dyes, and potato chips. All manufacturing, whether seeded with silicon wafers or not, will respond to network principles.

Consider oil—the quintessential atom-based resource. The classical theory of diminishing returns was practically invented to explain the oil industry. Easy oil is extracted cheaply at first; then at a certain point the expense of extraction doesn't justify the cost unless the price goes up. But by now the oil industry is so invaded by chip technology that it is beginning to obey the laws of the new economy. Sophisticated 3D viewing software allows geologists to map oil-yielding layers to within a few meters; computer-guided flexible drills can burrow sideways with precision, reaching small pockets of oil. Superior pumps extract more oil with less energy and maintenance. Diminishing returns are halted. The oil flows steadily at steady prices, as the oil industry slides into the new economy.

And what could be more industrial-age than automobiles? Yet, chips and networks can take the industrial age out of cars, too. Most of the energy a car consumes is used to move the car itself, not the passenger. So if the car's body and engine can be diminished in size, less power is needed to move the car, meaning the engine can be made yet smaller. A smaller engine requires a yet smaller engine, and so on down the slide of compounded value that microprocessors followed. The car's body can be reduced substantially using smart materials—stuff that requires increasing knowledge to invent and make—which in turn means a smaller, more efficient engine can power it.

Detroit and Japan have designed cars that weigh only 500 kilograms. Built out of ultra-lightweight composite fiber material, these prototypes are powered by high-tech hybrid engine motors. They reduce the mass of radiator, axle, and driveshaft by substituting networked chips. They insert chips to let the car self-diagnose its performance, in real time. They put chips in brakes, making them less likely to skid. They put microprocessors in the dashboard to ease navigation and optimize fuel use. They use hydrogen fuel cells that do not pollute, and electric motors with low noise pollution. And just as embedding chips in brakes made them better, these lightweight cars will be wired with network intelligence to make them safer: A crash will inflate intelligent multiple air bags—think "smart bubblepak."

The accumulated effect of this substitution of knowledge for material in automobiles is what energy visionary Amory Lovins, director of the Rocky Mountain Institute, calls a hypercar: an automobile that will be safer than today's car, yet can cross the continental United States on one tank of hydrogen fuel.

Already, the typical car boasts more computing power than your typical desktop PC. Already the electronics in a car cost more ($728) than the steel in the car ($675). But what the hypercar promises, says Lovins, is a car remade by silicon. A hypercar can be viewed as step toward a vehicle that is (and behaves like) a solid state module. A car becomes not wheels with chips, but a chip with wheels. And this chip with wheels will drive on a road system increasingly wired as a decentralized electronic network obeying the network economy's laws as well.

Once we visualize cars as chips with wheels, it's easier to imagine airplanes as chips with wings, farms as chips with soil, houses as chips with inhabitants. Yes, they will have mass, but that mass will be subjugated by the overwhelming amount of knowledge and information flowing through it. In economic terms, these objects will behave as if they had no mass at all. In that way, they migrate to the network economy.

Because information trumps mass, all commerce migrates to the network economy.

MIT Media Lab director Nicholas Negroponte guesstimates that the online economy will have reached $1 trillion by 2000. Most tenured economists think that figure is terribly optimistic. But actually that optimistic figure is terribly underestimated. It doesn't anticipate the scale on which the economic world will move on to the internet as the network economy infiltrates cars and traffic and steel and corn. Even if all cars aren't sold online immediately, the way cars are designed, manufactured, built, and operated will depend on network logic and chip power.

The current concern about the size of the online market will have diminishing relevance, because *all* commerce is jumping on to the internet. The distinctions between the network economy and the industrial economy will likewise blur and fade, as all economic activity is touched in some way by network rules. The key distinction remaining will be between the animated versus the inert.

The realm of the inert encompasses any object that is divorced from its economic information. A head of lettuce today for instance does not contain any financial information beyond a price sticker. Once applied, that price is fixed, too. It doesn't change unless a human changes it. The economic consequences of lettuce sales elsewhere, or a change in the general global economy do not affect the head of lettuce itself. Instead, lettuce-related information flows through wholly separate channels—news programs or business newsletters—that are divorced from the lettuce itself. The lettuce is economically inert.

The realm of the animated is different. It's vastly interconnected. In this coming world a head of lettuce carries its own identity and price, displayed perhaps on an LED slab nearby, or on a disposable chip attached to its stem. The price changes as the lettuce ages, as lettuce down the street is discounted, as the weather in California changes, as the dollar surges in relation to the Mexican peso. Traders back in supermarket headquarters manage the "yield" of lettuce prices using the same algorithms that airlines use to maximize their profits from airline seats. (An unsold seat on a 747 is as perishable as an unsold head of lettuce.) In relation to the net, the lettuce is animated. It is dynamic, adaptive, and interacting with events. A river of money and information flows through it. And if money and information flow through something, then it's part of the network economy.

The progression by which the old economy migrates toward the new follows a relentless logic:

- Increasing numbers of inert objects are animated by information networks.
- Once the inert is touched by a network, it obeys the rules of information.
- Networks don't retreat; they tend to multiply into new territories.
- Eventually all objects and transactions will run by network logic.

One is tempted to add "resistance is futile." The overwhelming long-term trend toward universal connection may seem Borg-like, as if all things will lose their identity and become part of one large mindless swarm. Two things should be made clear: 1) constant, ubiquitous connections do not per se eliminate individuality; and 2) by "all" I mean an ongoing trend that approaches an asymptote, not a finality.

One might say that industrialization eradicated hand-crafted production to the point where *all* objects are machine-made. That is true by and large, and it accurately describes the destination of a trend. But the trend has a few notable exceptions. In an era of objects made completely by machines, hand-made items are a scarcity and thus command very high prices. A few—but only a few—shrewd artisans and entrepreneurs can make a living crafting items by hand, items such as bicycles, furniture, guitars, that would ordinarily be stamped out in a factory. Resistance is marginal, but profitable.

The same will be true in the networking of the economy. Resistance will not be futile. In a world of ubiquitous connection, where everything is connected to everything else, scarce will be the person not connected at all, or the company not pushing ideas and intangibles. If these mavericks are able to interface with the networked economy without losing their distinctivness or value, then they will be sought out, and their products priced high. One can imagine a successful idea-artist in the year 2005 who does no email, no phone, no videoconferences, no VR, no books, and who does not travel. The only way to get her fabulous ideas is in person, face-to-face at her hideout, live. The fact that she is booked 8 months in advance only adds to her reputation.

MIT economist Paul Krugman has an alternative vision of how information technology will invert the expected order. He writes: "The time may come when most tax lawyers are replaced by expert systems software, but human beings are still needed—and well paid—for such truly difficult occupations as gardening, house cleaning, and the thousands of other services that will receive an ever-growing share of our expenditure as mere consumer goods become steadily cheaper." Actually we don't need to wait for the future. Recently I had to hire two different freelancers. One sat in her office moving symbols around. She transcribes tape-recorded interviews and charges $25 per hour. The other is a guy who works out of his home repairing greasy kitchen appliances. He charges $50 per hour, and as far as I could tell had more business of the two. Krugman's argument is that these "manual crafts" (as they are bound to be labeled when so high-priced) will level the salary discrepancies that now exist between high tech and low tech occupations.

My argument is that great gardeners will be high-priced not only because they are scarce and exceptions, but also because they, like everyone else, will be using technology to eliminate as much of the tedious repetitive work as possible, leaving them time to do what humans are so good at: working with the irregular and unexpected.

At the dawn of the industrial age it would have been difficult to imagine how such quintessential agrarian jobs as farming, husbandry, and forestry could become so industrialized. But that is what happened. Not just agrarian work, but just about every imaginable occupation of that period—especially menial labor—was intensely affected by industrialization. The trend was steady: The entire economy eventually became subjected to the machine.

The full-scale trend toward the network economy is equally hard to imagine, but its progression is steady. It follows a predictable pattern. The first jobs to be absorbed by the network economy are new jobs that could only exist in the new world: code hackers, cool hunters, webmasters, and Wall Street quants. Next to succumb are occupations with old goals that can be accomplished faster or better with new tools: real estate brokers, scientists, insurance actuaries, wholesalers, and anyone else who sits at a desk. Finally, the network economy engulfs all the unlikely rest—the butchers, bakers, and candlestick makers—until the entire economy is suffused by networked knowledge.

The three great currents of the network economy: vast globalization, steady dematerialization into knowledge, and deep, ubiquitous networking—these three tides are washing over all shores. Their encroachment is steady, and self-reinforcing. Their combined effect can be rendered simply: The net wins.

Strategies

Maximize the value of the network. Feed the web first. Networks are nurtured by making it as easy as possible to participate. The more diverse the players in your network—competitors, customers, associations, and critics—the better. Becoming a member should be a breeze. You want to know who your customers are, but you don't want to make it hard for them to get to you (IDs, yes; passwords, no). You want to make it easy for your competitors to join too (all their customers could potentially be yours as well). Be open to the power of network effects: Relationships are more powerful than technical quality. Especially beware of the "not-invented-here" syndrome. The surest sign of a great network player is its willingness to let go of its own standard (especially if it is "superior") and adopt someone's else's to leverage the network's effect.

Seek the highest common denominator. Because of the laws of plentitude and increasing returns, the most valuable innovations are not the ones with the highest performance, but the ones with the highest performance on the widest basis—the "highest per widest." Feeding the web first means ignoring state-of-the-art advances, and choosing instead the highest common denominator—the highest quality that is widely accepted. One practical reason to pick the highest-per-widest techniques and technologies is because complex technologies require passionate and informed users who can share experience and context, and you want the maximum dispersion of usage that doesn't sacrifice quality.

Don't invest in Esperanto. No matter how superior another way of doing something is, it can't displace an embedded standard—like English. Avoid any scheme that requires the purchase of brand new protocols when usable ones are widely adopted.

Apply an embedded standard in a new territory. Is there a way to accomplish what you want using existing standards and existing webs in a different context? Inventing a novel standard for an existing network is quixotic. But some of the greatest success stories in current times are about firms that master one network and then use its embedded standards to exploit an established network in need of improvement. This process is called "interfection." The present revolution in telephony is all about zealous internet firms that are interfecting the old Bell-head world of moving voices with newly established protocols for moving data on the internet (known as internet protocols, or IP). The huge increasing returns that spin off the internet give them a great advantage. Indeed, one telephony standard after another is falling before the relentless march of IP. Likewise, aggressive companies are leveraging the established desktop standard of Windows NT—with all its plentitude effects—to interfect new domains such as telephone switching gear. Even the huge cable TV networks have something to offer. The emerging standards for video transmission, such as MPEG, are trying to migrate onto the internet. In choosing which standard to back, consider dominant standards outside your current network that could interfect your own turf.

Animate it. As the network economy unfolds, more firms will begin to ask themselves this question: How do we put what we do into the logic of networks? How do we prepare a product to behave with network effects? How do we "netize" our product or service? (The answer is not "put it on a web site.") Architects, for instance, generate huge volumes of data. How can they be standardized? How can the data about a physical object (say a door) flow through or with that object? What are the fewest functions we can add to glass windows to incorporate them into networks? What steps can a contractor take to allow the networked flow of information from any architect to any contractor to any builder to any client? How do we increase the number of networks our service embraces?

Side with the net. Imagine that in 1960 an elf let you in on a secret: For the next 50 years computers would shrink drastically and cheapen yearly on a predictable basis. Subsequently, whenever you needed to make a technological decision, if you had counted on the smaller and cheaper, you would have always been right. Indeed you could have performed financial miracles knowing little more than this rule. Here is today's secret: In the coming 50 years, the net will expand and thicken yearly on a predictable basis—its value growing exponentially as it embraces more members, and its costs of transactions drop toward zero. Whenever you need to make a technological decision, if you err on the side of choosing the more connected, the more open system, the more widely linked standard, you will always be right.

Employ Evangelists. Economic webs are not alliances. There are often few financial ties among members of a web. An effective way of establishing standards and coordinating development is through evangelists. These are not salespeople, nor executives. Their job is simply to extend the web, to identify others with common interests and then assist in bringing them together. In the early days when Apple was a cocreator of the emerging PC web, it successfully employed evangelists to find third-party vendors to make plug-in boards, or to develop software for their machines. Go and do likewise.

6 LET GO AT THE TOP
After Success, Devolution

The tightly linked nature of the emerging economy makes it behave like a biological community. Wars and battles were the allegories of the industrial economy. Coevolution and infections are more apt in the new economy.

Companies are like organisms evolving in an ecosystem. Some ecosystems in nature offer few opportunities for life. In the Arctic there are only a couple of strategies for survival, and a species had better get good at one of them. Other biomes are chock-full of opportunities, which are in constant flux, appearing and disappearing as species jockey for their niches. The harmony we attribute to nature is not static perfection but a complex dance of ups, downs, trips and falls, and balance regained.

Rich, interactive, and highly flexible in shape, the network economy resembles a biome seething with action, a jungle in fast-forward motion. New niches open up constantly and vanish quickly. Competitors sprout beneath you and then gobble your spot up. One day you are king of the mountain, and the next day there is no mountain at all.

Biologists describe the struggle of an organism to adapt in this type of habitat as a long climb uphill, where uphill means greater adaptation. In this metaphor, an organism that is maximally adapted to the times is situated on a peak. Imagine a commercial organization instead of an organism. A company expends great effort to move its butt uphill, or to evolve its product so that it is sitting on top, maximally adapted to the consumer environment.

All organizations (profit and nonprofit alike) face two problems as they attempt to find their peak of optimal fit. Both problems are exacerbated by the constant turbulence of the network economy.

First, unlike the industrial era's relatively simple environment, in which it was fairly clear what an optimal product looked like and where on the stable horizon a company should place itself, it is increasingly difficult in the network economy to discern what hills are highest and which summits are false.

In biological terms, the new economic landscape is "rugged," disrupted by gulfs, precipices, and steep slopes. Trails are riddled with dead ends, lead to false summits, and made impassable by big-time discontinuities. Because the economic terrain is jumbled with no overall pattern, there is no certainty that a company intending to head up a slope toward a peak new market is actually climbing anything larger than a hill. In biospeak, they may succeed in getting to the top yet find themselves stuck on a suboptimal peak.

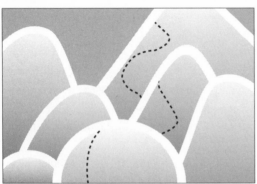

Turbulent times mean that local success is not global success. A company may be at peak efficiency, but on the wrong mountain. The trick is to select a high-potential area to excel in.

Big and small companies alike have to deal with their new landscape. It's often unclear whether a firm should strive to be on top of a mountain (for example, to be the world's most reliable hard disk manufacturer), when the whole mountain range beneath that particular peak may sink in a few years (if everyone moves their storage onto large protein arrays). An organization can cheer itself silly on its way to becoming the world's expert on a dead-end technology. (The nuclear power industry offers one example.)

Some of the most perfect technology was created just before its demise. Vacuum tube technology reached a nadir of complexity just before it vanished. As MIT economist James Utterback writes: "Firms are remarkably creative in defending their entrenched technologies, which often reach unimaginable heights of elegance in design and technical performance only when their demise is clearly predictable." It's relatively easy to arrive at a peak of perfection. The problem is that perfection can be local, or suboptimal, like being the best basketball player in your state, but unaware of national tournaments. While a firm is congratulating itself on creating the world's fastest punch card reader—the fastest in the universe!—the rest of the economic world has moved on to the PC.

The harsh news is that "getting stuck on a local peak" is a certainty in the new economy.

Instability and disequilibrium are the norms; optimazation won't last long. Sooner, rather than later, a product will be eclipsed at its prime. Indeed, an innovation at its prime increases its chances of being eclipsed. In *Mastering the Dynamics of Innovation*, a study of innovation in the automobile industry, Utterback concludes that "an unhappy byproduct of success in one generation of technology is a narrowing of focus and vulnerability to competitors championing the next technological generation." The product may be perfect, but for an increasingly smaller range of uses or customers.

While one product is perfecting its peak, an outsider can move the entire mountain by changing the rules. Detroit was the peak of perfection for big cars, but suddenly the small-car mountain overshadowed it. Sears was king of the retail mountain, but then Wal-Mart and Kmart's innovations created a whole new mountain range that towered above it. For a brief moment Nintendo owned the summits of the video-game mountain until Sega and later Sony built separate mountains even higher. Each of the displaced industries, companies, or products were stuck on a less optimal local peak.

There is only one way out. The stuck organism must devolve. In order to go from a peak of local success to another higher peak, it must first go downhill. To do that it must reverse itself and for a while become less adapted, less fit, less optimal. It must do business less efficiently, with less perfection, relative to its current niche.

This is a problem. Organizations, like living beings, are hardwired to optimize what they know—to cultivate success, not to throw it away. Companies find devolving unthinkable and impossible. There is simply no allowance in the enterprise for letting go.

And the better the company, the less room there is for devolution.

Everything about a modern organization is dedicated to pushing up-hill. The CEO is trained, and paid well, to push the firm toward the peak. Quality circles get the entire workforce marching uphill toward optimal performance. Consultants monitor the tiniest detail, trying to eliminate anything that might keep the company from attaining the peak of perfection. Reengineering wonks zero in on computer data showing which parts of the organization are lagging behind. Even the receptionist is in search of excellence.

Where in the modern company is the permission, let alone the skill, to let go of something that is working, and trudge downhill toward chaos?

And have no doubt: It will be chaotic and dangerous down below. The definition of lower adaptivity is that it places you closer to extinction. But you have to descend and risk extinction in order to have the opportunity to rise again.

Economist Joseph Schumpeter calls the progressive act of destroying success "creative destruction." It's an apt term. Letting go of perfection requires a brute act of will. And it can be done badly. Management guru Tom Peters claims that corporate leaders are now being asked to do two tasks—building up and then nimbly tearing down—and that these two tasks require such diametrically opposed temperaments that the same person cannot do both. He impishly suggests that a company in the fast-moving terrain of the network economy ordain a Chief Destruction Officer.

With or without someone in charge of creative destruction, there is no alternative (that we know of) to leaving behind perfectly good products, expensively developed technology, and wonderful brands, and heading down to trouble in order to ascend again with hope.

Once upon a time this march was rare. The relatively stable markets and technological environment of the industrial era were smooth, not rugged. Only a few parameters changed each year, and they changed gradually. Opportunities arrived with forewarning. Those days are over.

The biological nature of the new economic order means that the sudden disintegration of established domains will be as certain as the sudden appearance of the new.

There can be no expertise in innovation unless there is also expertise in demolishing the ensconced.

There is nothing wrong with perfection. To be maximally fit for a niche, to serve optimally, to seek the peak of perfection—these will always remain the goals of any firm, or individual. So why let go of perfection at the top?

The problem with the top is not too much perfection, but too little perspective. Great success in one product or service tends to block a longer, larger view of the opportunities available in the economy as a whole, and of the rapidly shifting terrain ahead. Legendary, long-lived companies are intensely outward-looking. They can spot a global peak and distinguish it from the many false peaks. They understand that an inward focus, especially a narrow focus on being "world's best" in some matter, can work against long-term adaptation by blinding the organization from seeking new heights. Better for the long haul is an outward perspective that is always seeking alternative mountains to climb.

This outward vista is all the more critical in the new economy because perfection is no longer a solo act. Success is a highly interdependent enterprise, encompassing a network of vendors, customers, and even competitors. A firm needs to explore widely, outside of the current favored position, and at times contrarily.

Letting go at the top is not an act against perfection, but against shortsightedness.

In addition to the scarcity of leaders willing to disassemble the profitable, and the natural bias of companies toward perfection, there is another reason why letting go is so hard. Economists Paul Milgrom and John Roberts studied the competencies—the winning traits—of a large number of firms in modern manufacturing and concluded that competencies of companies tended to occur in suites, or in a guilds of skills. This natural bundling of traits makes it very difficult for contenders to challenge a successful firm. As Richard Nelson, an economist at Columbia University says, "Successful firms often are difficult to imitate effectively because to do so requires that a competitor adopt a number of different practices at once." Companies can buy technology and human skills in a particular area. But gradually acquiring one or two competencies at a time does no good when you are attempting to displace a highly successful firm. The whole suite of mastery has to be acquired simultaneously in order for you to be competitively effective. A firm such as Disney is almost inimitable because of the difficulty of obtaining in one swift swoop its highly integrated mix of skills.

The natural bundling of traits also makes unraveling for devolution immensely difficult. To devolve demands going against all the best qualities of an organization all at once. The organic world offers a number of lessons in this regard. Biotechnology is built on the knowledge that most genes don't code for anything themselves. Most genes regulate—turn off and on—other genes. The genetic apparatus of a cell, then, is a dense network of hyperlinked interactions. Any gene is indirectly controlled by many other genes.

Thus, most attributes in a biological organism usually travel in the genome as loosely coupled associations. Blue eyes and freckles, say. Or red hair and a hot temper. Two important consequences follow from this. First, to get rid of the redhead's feisty temperament by evolution may also mean—at least at first—getting rid of the red hair. Animal breeders know this dilemma firsthand. It is difficult to breed out an unwanted trait without breeding out many desirable ones. Chicken breeders can't get rid of a chicken's aggressiveness without throwing out its egg-laying proficiencies.

Companies work the same way. The interlocking guild of competencies, which gives them their advantages, becomes a drawback during change. The increased interlinkage of the network economy heightens this dilemma. In the network economy, the skills of individual employees are more tightly connected, the activities of different departments more highly coordinated, the goals of various firms more independent. The net brings the influence of formerly unrelated forces to bear upon each potential move.

The more successfully integrated a firm's capabilities are, the harder it is to shift its expertise by changing just a little. Thus successful firms are more prone to failure during high rates of change. (Success makes it easy for the successful to deny this fact.) Indeed, the very success of successful organizations makes them conservative toward change—because they must unravel many interdependent skills—even if some are working fine.

The problem that IBM faced with the arrival of the personal computer in the early 1980s was not the problem of acquiring technological know-how. As a matter of fact, IBM already knew how to build personal computers better than anyone. But the package of proficiencies the blue suits had honed over the years to make IBM indomitable in the mainframe computer field could not be gradually adapted to fit the new faster-paced terrain of desktop-based computing. IBM was supreme in the old regime because their sales, marketing, R&D, and management skills were all optimally woven into a highly evolved machine. They couldn't change the size of the computers they sold without also altering their management, forecasting, and research skills at the same time. Changing everything at once is difficult for anyone, anytime.

Because skill guilds constrain (and defend) an organization, it is often far easier to start a new organization than to change a successful old one.

This is a major reason why the network economy is rich in start-ups. Starting new is a less risky way to assemble an appropriate new set of competencies than trying to rearrange an established firm, whose highly intertwined bundles resist unraveling.

In a rugged economic landscape, about the only hope an established company has for adapting to turbulent change is by employing the "skunk works" mode, which reflects another biological imperative. Computer simulations of evolution, particularly those run by David Ackely, a researcher at Bellcore, demonstrate how the source for mutations that eventually conquer a population start at the geographical fringes of the population pool. Then after a period of "beta testing" on the margins, the mutants overtake the center with their improvements and become the majority.

At the edges, innovations don't have to push against the inertia of an established order; they are mostly competing against other mutants. The edges also permit more time for a novel organism to work out its bugs without having to oppose highly evolved organisms. Once the mutants are refined, however, they sweep rapidly through the old order and soon become the dominant form.

This is the logic of skunk works. Hide a team far from the corporate center, where the clever can operate in isolation, away from the suffocating inertia of success. Protect the team from performance pressures until their work has had the kinks ironed out. Then introduce the innovation into the center. Every once in a while it will take over and become the new standard.

Economist Michael Porter surveyed 100 industries in 10 countries and found that in all the industries he studied, the source of innovations were usually either "outsiders" or else relative outsiders—established leaders in one industry making an entry into a new one.

To maximize innovation, maximize the fringes.

Encourage borders, outskirts, and temporary isolation where the voltage of difference can spark the new. The principle of skunk works plays a vital role in the network economy. By definition a network is one huge edge. It has no fixed center. As the network grows it holds increasing opportunities for protected backwaters where innovations can hatch, out of view but plugged in. Once fine-tuned, the innovation can replicate wildly. The global dimensions of the network economy means that an advance can be spread quickly and completely through the globe. The World Wide Web itself was created this way. The first software for the web was written in the relative obscurity of an academic research station in Geneva, Switzerland. Once it was up and running in their own labs in 1991, it spread within six months to computers all around the world.

The basic rules of success are eternal: serve customers obsessively, escalate quality, outdo your competitors, have fun. The nature of the new economy changes none of those rules. But the success they help one attain is not what it used to be. However you want to measure it, success is a type of inertia. The law of increasing returns can compound it but success still follows its momentum to the top—but the top is highly unstable now. Being at the top when the sands shift is a liability. For anyone sane, success should breed paranoia.

In the highly turbulent, quickly reforming environment of the new economy, the competitive advantage goes to the nimble and malleable, the flexible and quick. Speed and agility trump size and experience. Fast to find the new is only one half the equation; fast to let go is the other important half.

Of all the lessons that biology has to offer us as we begin to assemble a network economy, the necessity of abandoning our successes will be the hardest to practice.

Strategies

Don't mistake a clear view for a short distance. The terror of devolution is that a firm must remain intact while it descends into the harsh deserts between the mountains of successes. It must continue to be more or less profitable while it devolves. You can't jump from peak to peak. No matter how smart or how speedy an organization is, it can't get to where it wants to go unless it muddles across an undesirable place one step at a time. Enduring a period of less than optimal fitness is doubly difficult when a very clear image of the new perfection is in plain sight.

For instance, sometime in the early 1990s the Encyclopaedia Britannica company saw that they were stuck on a local peak. They were at the top: the best encyclopedia in print. They had a worldwide sales force peddling a world-recognized brand. But rising fast nearby was something new: CD-ROM. The outline of this dazzling new mountain was clear. Its height was inspiring. But it was a different realm from their old mountain: no paper, no door-to-door salespeople, cheap, little dinky disks on the shelf, and a media that required constant updates. They would have to undo much of what they knew. Still *there*, clear as could be, was their future. But while the destination was extremely clear, the path that led to it was treacherous. And, it turned out, the route was even longer than they thought. The company spent millions, lost salespeople in droves, and verged on collapse. They entered a scary period during which neither print nor CD worked. Eventually they completed the CD-ROM encyclopedia they had envisioned many years earlier, but only after an outsider (Microsoft) published a better one. Encyclopaedia Britannica's future is still in doubt. But their travails are common. Says futurist Paul Saffo: "We tend to mistake a clear view of the future for a short distance."

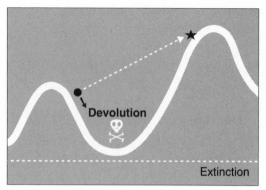

To scale a higher peak—a potentially greater gain—often means crossing a valley of less fitness first. A clear view of the future should not be mistaken for a short distance.

Today, nearly everyone in business has a clear view of the future of TV. It's something that comes to you in the same way you get the internet. You choose your shows, from 500 channels. You can shop, maybe interact with a game, or click for more information about a movie you are watching. The technology seems feasible, the physics logical, and the economics plausible. But Future TV looks a lot closer than it really is because the path between here and there winds through a barren desert with little optimal about it. Although the economics may work later, they barely work out now in the alkali flats. It may be that none of the large television or computer or phone companies are sufficiently nimble (or hungry) to make it across the valley of death—even though the shape of success is so visible.

Send the network out. There is only one sound strategy for crossing the valley: Don't go alone. Established firms are now doing what they should be doing: weaving dozens, if not hundreds, of alliances and partnerships; seeking out as many networks of affiliation and common cause as possible, sharing the risk by making a web. A motley caravan of firms can cross a suboptimal stretch with hope. Banding together buys their networks several things. First, it allows knowledge about the terrain to be shared. Some firm riding point might discover a small hill of opportunity. Settling there allows small oases of opportunity to be created. If enough intermediate oases can be found or made, the long journey can become a series of shorter hops along an archipelago of small successes. The more firms, customers, explorers, and vested interests that are attempting to cross, the more likely the archipelago can be found or created.

To create the future car—a car that is easily imaginable right now—an entrepreneurial car company can only succeed by spinning together a network of vendors, regulators, insurers, road makers, and competitors to help others to devolve quickly and cross.

Who is in charge of devolution? It is a rare leader who can creatively destroy as well as relentlessly build. It's a rare committee that will vote to terminate what works. It's a rare outsider whose advice to relinquish a golden oldie will be heeded. You are in charge of devolving. Everyone is. It's just one more chore in the network economy.

Question success. Not every success needs to be abandoned drastically, but every success needs to be questioned drastically. Do interesting substitutes exist? Are radical alternatives receiving compounding attention? You need to consider innovations far afield, ones that are not "on the same mountain." Are there innovations that are changing the rules of the game? Beware of minor incremental improvements—slight baby steps on the same mountain. These can be a form of denial. Nicholas Negroponte, director of the MIT Media Lab, declares "Incrementalism is innovation's worst enemy."

Searching as a way of life. In the network economy, nine times out of ten, your fiercest competitor will not come from your own field. In turbulent times, when little is locked in, it is imperative to search as wide as possible for places where innovations erupt. Innovations increasingly interfect from other domains. A ceaseless blanket search—wide, easy, and shallow—is the only way you can be sure you will not be surprised. Don't read trade magazines in your field; scan the magazines of other trades. Talk to anthropologists, poets, historians, artists, philosophers. Hire some 17-year-olds to work in your office. Make a habit to visit a web site at random. Tune in to talk radio. Take a class in scenario making. You'll have a much better chance at recognizing the emergence of something important if you treat these remote venues as neighbors.

7 FROM PLACES TO SPACES
Making a Different Kind of Big

"Geography is dead!"

This pronouncement has become a cliche among the advocates of digitalization and telecommunications. The advent of universal and inexpensive communication is said to usher in an era where distance, place, real estate, and geography are irrelevant. The notion is only half true.

Place still matters, and will for a long time to come. However, the new economy operates in a "space" rather than a place, and over time more and more economic transactions will migrate to this new space.

Geography and real estate, however, will remain, well . . . real. Cities will flourish, and the value of a distinctive place, such as a wilderness area, or a charming hill village, will only increase.

Tom Peters, the perennially entertaining management guru, likes to scare the daylights out of dazed American CEOs by proclaiming, "Think of Asia, Latin America, Eastern Europe! They're smart, fast, and cheap. And they're next door. Your worst nightmare of a competitor is now only one-eighth of a second away!" That's the maximum time it takes a signal to travel from one end of the globe to the other. These hungry competitors can do anything you can do, cheaper, and they all are, at most, only an eighth of a second away. In short, Peters proclaims the death of distance and the arrival of globalization.

That's the bad news. The good news is that those geographically far away competitors will never be any closer than an eighth of a second. And for many things in life, that is too far away.

A kiss for instance. Or playing sports. Or getting to know flowers.

Start-up companies selling futuristic multiplayer online games have dis-covered that the inherent delay in the speed of light circling the globe causes real-time experiences to fail. That noticeable gap makes no real difference in the transmission of a book order, or a weather signal, but enough of life thrives on subtle instantaneous responses that one-eighth of a second kills intimacy and spontaneity. Thus actual real-time face-to-face meetings will retain their irreplaceable value. Thus airline travel will increase as fast as online communication increases. Thus cities will endure as lag-free places where there are no one-eighth second delays.

People will inhabit places, but increasingly the economy inhabits a space.

A place is bounded by four dimensions. For two things to be adjacent, they must be close to each other on one of four axes: up/down, left/right, back/forth (x, y, z), and time. As rich as physical places are (and we still don't appreciate how rich they can be), they limit the number of connec-tions that entities can make within them. A person in a place can only in-teract with a fixed and rather small number of other people in the same vicinity. Artifacts can touch only the other artifacts in close proximity.

A space, unlike a place, is an electronically created environment. It is where more and more of the economy happens. Unlike place, space has unlimited dimensions. Entities (people, objects, agents, bits, nodes, etc.) can be adjacent in a thousand different ways and a thousand different direc-tions. A person in an electronic space can communicate to 10 million peo-ple at once, or interact in a game with 20,000 others—things that would be

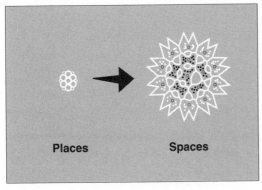

Places   **Spaces**

The invention of communication allowed life to evolve from globular organisms into fantastic beings, just as networks allow place-based firms to blossom into fantastic spaces.

impossible in physical space. An automobile can be linked in hundreds of directions—to other cars stuck in traffic miles away, environmental monitors, satellite navigation antennas, toll collectors, and the manufacturer's engine-performance center. In physical place a car can only interact with those within braking distance of its front and rear bumpers.

Spaces aren't bound by proximity. The advantage of spaces is rooted less in their nongeographical virtuality and more in their unlimited ability to absorb connections and relationships. By means of communications, network spaces can connect all kinds of nodes, dimensions, relationships, and interactions—not just those physically close to one another.

The popular suffix of "space" is a truncated version of cyberspace, a science fiction term for an immersive electronic space. But the roots of the term are deeper. The technical concept of "space" came out of mathematics and computer science. Space is one way scientists describe complex systems; very complex spaces have their own unique dynamics. The notation of space is particularly handy when describing the ordinarily vague and indefinite form of networks. The net, as it encompasses billions of objects and agents (there are already more than 100,000 cameras on the net), operates in what mathematicians call "very high dimensions," and has correspondingly novel dynamics. As electronic mediated environments expand, place has less influence and complex space more. As the economy infiltrates each network medium, it trades a physical marketplace for a conceptual *marketspace*.

The network economy shifts places to spaces.

In the new realm of high dimensional spaces, the network economy exhibits the following space-based behaviors.

- A different kind of bigness
- Rampant clustering
- Peer authority
- Re-intermediation

The industrial economy made it impossible to live next door to the source of all the goods consumers desired. If you wanted bananas, many intermediaries had to handle the fruit between the plantation in Honduras and your kitchen. Between the author of a book and you there needed to be a chain of editors, bankers, printers, distributors, wholesalers, and booksellers. Between you and good health care were doctors, nurses, insurance behemoths, and hospital staff. Between you and the car of your dreams stood a line of miners, smelters, engineers, manufacturers, railroad yards, showrooms, and salesmen. Each one of these agents moved the good or service along; some by completing the product (the car engineer) or customizing the service (the hospital staff), and some simply by physically moving it toward you (the banana boat). In business theory this line came to be known as the value chain. Each intermediate link in the long chain of creation added some measure of extra value, justifying the cost the link added to the good's final price. Companies competed to insert themselves into a value chain, then to expand their control of greater lengths of the chain.

One of the very first noticeable effects of computers and networked communications was the alarming way they disrupted traditional value chains. Futurist Paul Saffo calls the multiple interactions needed to survive in the new economy a move "from value chain to value web."

In the marketspace of networks, value flows in webs.

Many classic value chains were crowded with intermediaries who distributed a completed product or service. Take the banana wholesalers. Although they physically handled the product and often stored it in inventory at great cost, their primary value to the customer was informational. In theory, small bunches of bananas could be wrapped and sent directly to your home from a particular plantation with fewer intermediaries involved in warehousing and storage, and thus at lower costs. You would place an order directly to Best Bananas in Honduras for one bunch per week, except during the school holidays, and they then would mail them out to you. To do that effectively, though, would require network technology capable of a) finding a plantation you like; b) getting the right bunch to you at the right time; c) shifting to a cooperating planter if the first planter's fruit was not yet ripe; d) tracking the account payable for such a tiny buyer as yourself; and, e) dealing with all the millions of ordinary exceptions and screw-ups that any system as complex as this would entail.

The industrial age had no technology capable of doing that, so it substituted the wholesale system for networked information. Orders were aggregated at the local produce stand, sent to a wholesaler, who aggregated them further, and relayed the combined request through various shipping intermediaries to a farmers' coop, which distributed orders to various planters. Your personal "order" was submerged in a sea of others; the system essentially ignored it. Making their way back to you, the bananas followed a reverse chain of links, sitting in warehouses as a way to buffer the incomplete consumer information they should have had.

It may be a long while before bananas skip the industrial value chain, but other foods, higher priced and not as bulky, already can be bought this way. Food fanatics in cities anywhere can purchase specialty coffees, or authentic maple syrup, or organic beef by linking up with farmers directly and getting their goods right from the farm via the post office, or FedEx networks, bypassing the wholesale and retail intermediaries. When gourmets use web sites and direct-mail catalogs to buy directly from growers, the traditional intermediaries are taken out of the picture.

The banking industry was the first to name this creeping displacement of intermediaries. They noticed, quite rightly, that as information technology infiltrated the banking industry, and as the industry was deregulated, nobody seemed to need banks anymore—at least not banks as bureaucratic intermediaries. You could get easier loans at Sears, higher interest from a mutual fund, and better service at an ATM. Banking functions were being "*dis*intermediated" the bankers cried! For the typical neighborhood bank this was especially true. The disintermediation of the financial systems continues unabated; every week another bank branch shuts down.

As more commercial activities shift toward knowledge and information, the economy seems ripe for fatal disintermediation. Why should such digital age products as music CDs and news reports travel any other route except the short one that proceeds directly from the artist or author to you, the listener? Recent success stories, such as the case of Matt Drudge, give credence to a network's inclination to bypass the middle guys. Drudge, a no-name Hollywood gossip reporter, dispatched his insider scoops directly from a bedroom computer to a growing list of web readers until he had a national readership and a national brand. Some bands, both famous and unknown, are attempting the same thing in music.

The laborious tasks of stamping out disks, storing them, trucking them across country, warehousing on pallets, and then fighting for display space in a music store all seem to evaporate as network technologies make the transmission of music to fans direct and short. Big net, no middlemen, no fuss.

The potential of disintermediation, however, looms larger than the actuality at the moment, and casts a large and frightening shadow. Retailers, especially, are in a panic. If anyone can log on to the web and comparison shop for the lowest-priced refrigerator directly from the manufacturer, what's in it for the mall stores? If anyone can order up a video from the studio, what's in it for the local video shop? If anyone can get 5,000 sitcoms on demand, who needs NBC? The wholesalers are worried silly, but artists and creators are euphoric. The web promised (finally!) a way to beat the system of limited shelf space that stymied the debut of new novels, new albums, and new products in every type of store. With the web, there was unlimited shelf space. There was success in store for everyone!

When *Wired* magazine began developing one of the very first commercial web sites in 1993, the phrase "unlimited shelf space" was often used by potential contributors. Closely linked to this phrase was "bypassing the editor": the notion that editors were superfluous intermediaries, and that writers and readers didn't have to be subject to the frustrating and degrading filtering of go-betweeners. The raw stuff would flow in its full length and naked power directly from writer to reader. Our first prototypes convinced us that that wasn't how the net worked. The web site we launched and continue to build today (*Wired Digital*) is based on a different premise: that in a network economy, intermediaries have tremendous value.

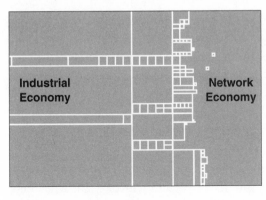

Technology encourages the proliferation of intermediates. Smaller companies, in greater numbers, are able to find niches where niches could not have existed before.

Everything about the web, especially the over 1 million web sites currently in existence, suggests that the expectation that the network economy favors disintermediation is exactly wrong. It is quite the opposite. Network technologies do not eliminate intermediaries. They spawn them. Networks are a cradle for intermediaries.

Everywhere networks go, intermediaries follow. The more nodes, the more middlemen.

It is so cheap to complete a transaction from almost anywhere, anytime, that tiny slivers of value, built upon microcosts of transactions, can be surgically inserted into all manner of processes and products. Because each microvalue sliver is so cheap, there is economic room for multiple microvalue slivers where before there was only room for one intermediary. As transaction costs plummet to the nanopenny level, some little crumb of value can be profitably added to more and more processes.

The combinatorial mathematics of networks also boost the opportunities for intermediaries. By definition, every node on a network is a node *between* other nodes. The more connections there are between members in a net, the more intermediary nodes there can be. Everything in a network is intermediating something else.

All nodes in a network are intermediaries.

Someday everyone in the world will have email, and when they do, I don't want six billion emails a day as everyone shares what's on their mind. Since half the world will probably have their own businesses, and half of those will be start-ups, I will do everything I can to insert intermediaries between my mailbox and their mailsenders, to sort out, route, and filter my incoming mail. By the same token when I go to email old Mohammed Jhang, someone whom I have not met, who lives in Chinese Turkestan, to let him know about my latest gene therapy cure for arthritis, I'll need an intermediary to find him and then to reach past his blocking filters. I probably won't get through so I'll need more intermediaries (An advertiser? A lottery? A locating agent?) to lure him into the open, perhaps a pigeon-racing club, or the cineplex where he gets his movies from, to make him aware of my discovery. Sure, anyone can type "new gene therapy cure for arthritis" and turn up 32,000 hits. But you need intermediaries to vouch for their medical worthiness. You need intermediaries to compare my price and the others.

The marketspace of the new economy can hold far more intermediaries than the marketplace of the old could. This swelling bulk of intermediaries becomes an exaggerated middle. As networks proliferate, so do overlapping clusters of intersecting interests that reside in the realm of the middle. In fact the hypermiddle is less a size than a shape.

Technology has always influenced the size of companies. The invention of the elevator made possible high-rise buildings, which brought thousands of employees together into one tightly coupled physical space. High-rise towers launched the golden era of the centralized corporation. The advent of telephones on employee desks allowed the centralized corporation to spawn branches in neighboring cities and states, so that corporations grew in staff; at its peak in 1967 GM employed some 850,000 people in all of its factories and administration buildings.

Computers and networking technology initiated a shift in the other direction. What took 8 people before might be done now with 7 using technology. Firms that relied heavily on these technologies could reduce the number of employees. A company like Microsoft today employs a relatively meager 20,000 people.

If firms got smaller with tiny doses of networking technology, then the logical extrapolation dictated that with large doses the firm should continue to reduce until it reached one employee. Some statistics tend to confirm this drift. Counting the 14 million self-employed, the 8.3 million independent contractors, and the 2.6 million temporarily employed

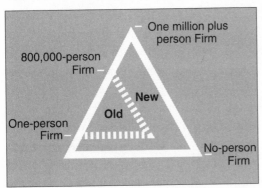

Network technology increases the size of the largest firms yet makes it more possible to have smaller firms while also increasing the number of midsize firms.

in the United States, there are 25 million Americans today working as a unit of one. If this trend continues for a couple more decades, in the future everyone will be a free-agent working for themselves, and our country will be a free-agent nation.

But network power cuts both ways. Although networks empower the solo practitioner, they also empower very large organizations. We are just as likely to see the rise of the Godzilla-nation as the free-agent nation. Big has not really been done yet. With the incredible place-shifting power of communication technologies, and a yet-to-be-tapped global market, the world will soon witness corporations that will dwarf the size of the old GM. One can imagine a truly global consultancy, such as Andersen Consultants or Ernst & Young, having a staff of one million worldwide.

But the big will have a different kind of bigness.

In the space of networks, size is reckoned differently. The new organization is flat, spread out laterally, diffuse, with nested cores, and swollen in the middle. Companies will change shape more than they will change size.

During the industrial era, size was polarized to extremes. There was the "world," or the masses, and there was "I." Industrialization emphasized the large-scale efficiencies of mass production, which quickly led to mass consumption and mass society. A drift to the large, if not the largest, coursed through the society. If something was worth doing well, it was worth doing at the scale of the world. Ambitions ran to the tallest skyscraper, the biggest factory, the largest dam, the longest bridge. The technologies of communication of that age also flexed the muscle of big. The printed page and the radio signal—as central to the industrial age as anything made of iron—informed, educated, and mobilized hundreds of millions from a single transmission source. The power of big was never so nicely diagrammed as in the TV: a tiny spark amplified to reach billions of people over thousands of miles at once, in unison.

The "I" on the other hand was fed by mass advertising and the cult of the individual, which sprang up after the Second World War. A fascination with psychoanalysis, with the ego, with personal expression and self-esteem, culminated in the "Me decades" starting in the 1970s. The first bits of the information age fed this whetted appetite for further individualism. We got personal computers amid personal trainers, personal advisers, and expectations of everything personalized.

Left behind by industrialization was the realm of the middle. The middle was once where everyone lived and most things happened. This size once flourished in geographical towns (with tens of thousands), ordinary communities (with thousands) and neighborhoods (with hundreds). Places embraced the middle very well.

But the vitality of places was weakened by a bifurcating pressure to make things either huge for the masses or solo for the personal. The logic of the modern was: it must appeal to everyone, or to only me. Neither mass society nor the cult of the personal was equipped to deal with the peculiar dynamics of the middle. There was little economic or technological support for aiming an innovation at 5,000 people. Neither broadcast nor the personal chip, for example, really knew how to do towns and neighborhoods.

The network economy encourages the middle space. It supplies technology (which the industrial age could not) to nurture mid-sized wonders.

Technology for mass production will remain. Technology to customize the personal will accelerate. But for the first time we have technology naturally suited for a size smaller than mass and greater than the self. We have a technology of net and web, stuffed with middleness.

Futurist Alvin Toffler says it best: "The era of mass society is over." He ticks off the casualties: "No more mass production. No more mass consumption. No more mass education. No more mass democracy. No more weapons of mass destruction. No more mass entertainment."

In its place: a world of demassified niches. Niche production, niche consumption, niche diversion, niche education. Niche world. Communities. Affinity groups. Clubs. Special Interest Groups. Clans. Subcultures. Tribes. Cults. (There is nothing utopian about this world.) Instead of the mass technology of broadcast TV, we now have net-centric alternatives.

We see the problem of the unserved middle most clearly in communication media. Say you wanted to talk to 10,000 people once a day. Unless you wanted to speak to a group bounded by geography—a small town, or a subset of a small city—you'd be stymied. You can broadcast to a million unknowns hoping you happen to catch some of the 10,000 you want, or you can slowly collect the names of individuals who contact you, one by one, and transmit to them directly. Neither way is elegant. Retailers call this the "hard middle," because it is so hard to service a group of 10,000 customers who share a common interest but not a common geography. Retailers crave the middle because they have learned that you can't appeal to folks with a simple naked exchange of money. You need other essentials of marketplaces—conversations, loitering, flirting, people-watching. Before you can have commerce, you need a community, a middle number of interacting people.

It takes a village to make a mall. Community precedes commerce.

The hard middle is a pervasive problem. We have tools to access the ideas in one person's book: its index and table of contents. We have tools to access the ideas of a library of millions of books: its card catalog. But we don't have tools to access ideas in the hard middle, the region of expertise in 10,000 scholars, or 1,000 books. Where do you go for a listing of key words, key subjects, and key ideas for the complete literature about the U.S. Civil War?

Until recently, nowhere. Today, the symbol WWW immediately pops into our mind. We see in the World Wide Web the promise of creating a viable midlands. In this particular case the hyperlinking of all documents could be filtered and categorized to generate an index to middle-sized knowledge.

The electronic space encourages middle communities. Unlike either

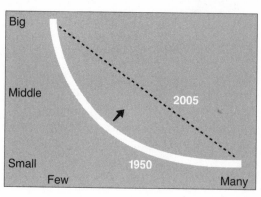

Services and goods for previously ignored community- and town-sized groups, also known as the hard middle, can make economic sense with network technology.

broadcast or PC chips, a network fosters the energy that flows from the friend of a friend to the friend of a friend. Network architecture can find, cultivate, persuade, manage, and nourish intermediate-sized audiences and communities focused on common interests. Niche markets, in other words. Magazines, rooted in the postal system *network*, have served niche markets for a century. But the emerging broadband network offers many relationships the postal network (and magazines) could not: spontaneous reply, fully symmetrical bandwidth, true peerage communication, archives, filtering, community memory, etc.

Network logic supports the middle space in several ways.

First, the plunging costs of information make it possible to find, then connect, two passions together far more efficiently than in the past. Once connected, cheap transactions keep the connection flourishing.

Second, symmetrical messaging, text, video, audio, 3D spaces, archives, privacy controls, all enhance the once slim attractions of a virtual community experience, keeping the community longer.

Third, the ubiquity of e-money in the network means that every niche has the ability to initiate an indigenous economy. The knowledge that dog breeders used to swap among themselves can become lucrative to the community as a whole when plugged into the network economy.

Fourth, the border-collapsing nature of the network economy means embryonic communities can theoretically draw upon a larger pool of potential members: all 6 billion humans. The law of increasing returns can feed a small interest into a mid-sized interest. Whereas once there was a lone fanatic for every notion, now there is a devoted web site for every fanatic notion; soon there can be 10,000 fellow enthusiasts for every fascination.

The network economy has set into motion the power of hobby tribes and informed peers. Amateurs, plugged into the net, discover comets, find fossils, and track bird migrations better than pros. By networking their interests and passing tips around, amateurs also create software in languages so new that they are taught in no classrooms. These self-organized communities, unleashed from their obscurity by the net, are the new authorities.

Silent movie buffs and meteorite collectors are quickly gathering on the net because the net's space coheres them into a middle market, served at last by business and sales aimed directly at them. Egyptologists or cancer patients can create a mid-sized agora (neither insignificant nor huge) for ideas and knowledge. There was no place in mass markets for the niche communities of ethnic tribes or Klingon speakers, but the network economy constructs a space for them.

But mass broadcast TV and big print publishing are not going away. The chief advantage of peerage networks—that information flows in ripples through a web of equal nodes—is also the chief weakness of networks. Information can only advance by indirect osmosis, passing along like gossip. The web becomes a thicket of obstacles preventing simultaneous dissemination to all parts.

The net shifts from mass media to mess media.

On the new mess media, rumor, conspiracy, and paranoia run rampant. These have always been the downsides of communities; network midlands will also have to learn to deal with impenetrable webs and paranoic sensibilities. Capitalizing on these disadvantages, broadcast will thrive symbiotically within the network economy. Sometimes real-time signals en masse are needed and wanted. Broadcast's flyover will be used, or material will be directly pushed to users. The web needs broadcast to focus attention, and broadcast needs the web to find communities.

Network technology expands all sizes. It enables the biggest to become bigger and the smallest to become smaller. In the near future we can expect to see institutions larger than they have ever been, and smaller than they have ever been. For instance, a few banks will grow monstrously large at the same time that other banks shrink to the size of a smart card in a wallet and increase their numbers by millions. The middle expands, too. That hard-to-reach territory that once was well served by places is rejuvenated.

The space of network nodes and flows creates new social organizations, new forms of companies, in oddball sizes, and in unconventional arrangements. We are on the brink of entering a world where almost any shape of business is possible.

Strategies

The only side a network has is outside. Like a rapidly spinning galaxy, the net creates an unrelenting force that sends everything from the inside toward the outer edges. Since little is left inside, the action is thrown to the perimeter. Rather than buck this centripetal force, companies should consider outsourcing chores to other equally amorphous networked companies. The most powerful capitulation to the net's outward spin is to outsource seemingly core activities. For instance, some airline companies outsource the business of air-freight hauling, even though the cargo is carried by their own planes. There are 1,001 reasons why core outsourcing can't be done, but 999 of them ignore the centripetal force of the network economy.

Prepare for flash crowds. Electronic spaces unhinge a crowd of visitors: They can appear in a flash and then leave in a flash. During the chess match between Deep Blue and Gary Kasparov, the IBM web site welcomed 5 million visitors. When the match was over the site was empty. On the eve of the 1996 U.S. elections, the CNN web site experienced 50 million attempts to log on. The next day, the crowd was gone. One day a flash crowd is pounding at the doors, the next day they have vanished. The mass audience has transformed itself into a wave that swishes around from one hot spot to another. But the nature of spaces is that in order to accommodate a flash crowd when they do come, you have to be ready, tooled up.

8 NO HARMONY, ALL FLUX
Seeking Sustainable Disequilibrium

In the industrial perspective, the economy was a machine that was to be tweaked to optimal efficiency, and once finely tuned, maintained in productive harmony. Companies or industries especially productive of jobs or goods had to be protected and cherished at all costs, as if these firms were rare watches in a glass case.

As networks have permeated our world, the economy has come to resemble an ecology of organisms, interlinked and coevolving, constantly in flux, deeply tangled, ever expanding at its edges. As we know from recent ecological studies, no balance exists in nature; rather, as evolution proceeds, there is perpetual disruption as new species displace old, as natural biomes shift in their makeup, and as organisms and environments transform each other.

Even the archetypal glories of hardwood forests or coastal wetlands, with their apparent wondrous harmony of species, are temporary federations on the move. Harmony in nature is fleeting. Over relatively short periods of biological time, the mix of species churns, the location of ecosystems drift, and the roster of animals and plants changes as they come and go.

So it is with network perspective: companies come and go quickly, careers are patchworks of vocations, industries are indefinite groupings of fluctuating firms.

Change is no stranger to the industrial economy or the embryonic information economy; Alvin Toffler coined the term "future shock" in 1970 as the reasonable response of humans to an era of accelerating change.

But the network economy has moved from change to flux.

Change, even in its shocking forms, is rapid difference. Flux, on the other hand, is more like the Hindu god Shiva, a creative force of destruction and genesis. Flux topples the incumbent and creates a platform for more innovation and birth. This dynamic state might be thought of as "compounded rebirth." And its genesis hovers on the edge of chaos.

Donald Hicks of the University of Texas studied the half-life of Texan businesses for the past 22 years and found that their longevity has dropped by half since 1970. That's change. But Austin, the city in Texas in which new businesses have the shortest expected life spans, also has the fastest-growing number of new jobs and the highest wages. That's flux.

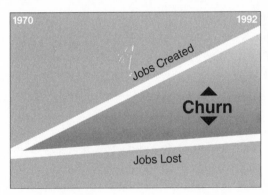

The number of old jobs lost increases, but not as fast as the number of new jobs created. More important, the spread of gained jobs over lost jobs widens.

Hicks told his sponsors in Texas that "the vast majority of the employers and employment on which Texans will depend in the year 2026 — or even 2006 — do not yet exist." In order to produce 3 million new jobs by 2020, 15 million new jobs must be created in all, because of flux. "Rather than considering jobs as a fixed sum to be protected and augmented, Hicks argued, the state should focus on encouraging economic churning — on continually recreating the state's economy," writes Jerry Useem in *Inc.*, a small-business magazine that featured Hick's report. Ironically, only by promoting flux can long-term stability be achieved.

When flux is inhibited, slow death takes over. Contrast Texas and the other 49 states with the European Union. Between 1980 and 1995 Europe protected 12 million governmental jobs, and in the process of fostering stasis lost 5 million jobs in the private sector. The United States, fostering flux, saw a staggering 44 million old jobs disappear from the private sector. But 73 million new jobs were generated, for a net gain of 29 million, and in the process the United States kept its 12 million government jobs, too. If you can stand the turmoil, flux triumphs.

This notion of constant flux is familiar to ecologists and those who manage large networks. The sustained vitality of a complex network requires that the net keep provoking itself out of balance.

If the system settles into harmony and equilibrium, it will eventually stagnate and die.

Innovation is disruption; constant innovation is perpetual disruption. This seems to be the goal of a well-made network: to sustain a perpetual disequilibrium. A few economists studying the new economy (among them Paul Romer and Brian Arthur) have come to similar conclusions. Their work suggests that robust growth sustains itself by poising on the edge of constant chaos. "If I have had a constant purpose it is to show that transformation, change, and messiness are natural in the economy," writes Arthur.

The difference between chaos and the edge of chaos is subtle. Apple Computer, in its attempt to seek persistent disequilibrium and stay innovative, may have tottered too far off-balance and let itself unravel toward extinction. Or, if its luck holds, it may discover a new mountain to ascend after a near-death experience.

The dark side of flux is that the new economy builds on the constant extinction of individual companies as they're outpaced or morphed into yet newer companies in new fields. Industries and occupations also experience this churn. Even a sequence of rapid job changes for workers—let alone lifetime employment—is on its way out. Instead, careers—if that is the word for them—will increasingly resemble networks of multiple and simultaneous commitments with a constant churn of new skills and outmoded roles. About 20% of the American workforce already have an arrangement other than the traditional employee relationship with one employer. And 86% of them claim to be happy about it.

Nowhere is this trend toward constant flux more evident than in the entertainment industry centered in southern California. Hollywood's "cultural-industrial complex" includes not just film, but also music, multimedia, theme park design, TV production, and commercials.

Giant film studios no longer make movies. Loose entrepreneurial networks of small firms make movies, which appear under the names of the big studios. In addition to various camera crews, about 40 to 50 other firms, plus scores of freelancers, connect up to produce a movie; these include special effects vendors, prop specialists, lighting technicians, payroll agencies, security folks, and catering firms. They convene as one financial organization for the duration of the movie project, and then when the movie is done, the company disperses. Not too much later they will reconvene as other movie-making entities in entirely new ad hoc arrangements. Cyberpunk author Bruce Sterling has his own inimitable way of describing the flux of "Hollywood film ad-hocracies." To make a movie, he says, "You're pitchforking a bunch of freelancers together, exposing some film, using the movie as the billboard to sell the ancillary rights, and after the thing gets slotted to video, everybody just vanishes."

Fewer than ten entertainment companies employ more than 1,000 employees. Of the 250,000 people involved in the entertainment complex in the Los Angeles region, an estimated 85% of the firms employ 10 people or fewer. Joel Kotkin, author of a landmark 1995 article in *Inc.* magazine entitled, "Why Every Business Will Be Like Show Business," writes: "Hollywood has mutated from an industry of classic huge, vertically integrated corporations into the world's best example of a network economy. Eventually, every knowledge-intensive industry will end up in the same flattened, atomized state. Hollywood just has gotten there first."

Silicon Valley is not far behind. The ICE businesses — information, communication, and entertainment — all rely on speed and flexibility to survive in a self-made speedy and flexible environment. Things move so fast that even a corporation — any corporation — seems too rigid and staid. You can't alter bureaucratic structure fast enough, so don't even build one to begin with.

Networks are immensely turbulent and uncertain. The prospect of constantly tearing down what is now working will make future shock seem tame. As creatures of habit we will challenge the need to undo established successes. We are sure to find exhausting the constant, fierce birthing of so much that is new. The network economy is so primed to generate self-making newness that we may experience this ceaseless tide of birth as a type of violence.

In a poetic sense, the prime goal of the new economy is to undo— company by company, industry by industry—the industrial economy.

In reality, of course, the industrial cortex cannot be undone. But a larger web of new, more agile, more tightly linked organizations can be woven around it. These upstart firms bank on constant change and flux.

Change itself is no news, however. Ordinary change triggers yawns. Most change is mere churn, a random disposable newness that accomplishes little. Churn is the status quo for these times. At the other extreme, there is change so radical that it topples the tower. Like inventions that fail because they are way ahead of their times, it is possible to reach too far with change.

What the network economy coaxes forth is a selective flux. The right kind of change, in the right doses. In almost all respects this kind of change is what we mean by innovation.

The world "innovation" is so common now that its true meaning is hidden. A truly innovative step is neither too staid and obvious, nor too far out. The innovative step is change that is neither random directionless churn, nor so outrageous that it can't be appreciated. We wouldn't properly call just another variation of something an innovation. We also wouldn't call a shift to something that only worked in theory, but not practice, or that required a massive change in everyone else's behavior to work, an innovation.

A real innovation is sufficiently different to be dangerous. It is change just this side of being ludicrous. It skirts the edge of the disaster, without going over. Real innovation is scary. It is anything but harmonious.

The selective flux of innovation permeates the network economy the way efficiency permeated the industrial economy. The innovative flux is not merely dedicated to devising more interesting products, although that is its everyday chore. Innovation and flux saturate the entire emerging space of the new economy. Innovation premiers in:

New products
New categories of products

New methods to make old and new products
New types of organizations to make products
New industries
New economies

All of these will twist and turn as change, dangerous change, spirals through them. This is why there is such a maniacal fuss about innovation. When management gurus drone on about the imperative of innovation, they are right. Firms still need excellence, quality of service, reorganization, and real time, but nothing quite embodies the ultimate long-term task in this new economy as the tornado of innovation.

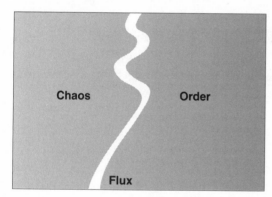

Because large systems must tread a path between the ossification of order and the destruction of chaos, networks tend to be in a constant state of turmoil and flux.

This is where life lives, between the rigid death of planned order and the degeneration of chaos. Too much change can get out of hand, and too many rules—even new rules—can lead to paralysis. The best systems have this living quality of few rules and near chaos. There is enough binding agreement between members that they don't fall into anarchy, yet redundancy, waste, incomplete communications, and inefficiency are rife.

My own involvement in groups that launched successful change, and my secondhand knowledge of many, many others involved in world-changing innovation, convinces me that all of these ensembles teetered on the brink of chaos at their peak performance. Whatever front they put up to the public or investors, behind the scenes most of the group ran around screaming "It's pathologically out of control here!" Every organization is dysfunctional to some degree, but innovative organizations, in their moment of glory, tend to slide toward uncoordinated communication, furious bouts of genius, and life-threatening disorganization. Everyone involved swears they will institute just enough structure to prevent flameout in the future, but I've never seen radical innovation emerge from an outfit that wasn't halfway to unraveling at the epicenter of change. Most of the studies of optimal evolution in complex systems confirm this view. The price for progressive change in maximum doses is a dangerous (and thrilling) ride to the edge of disruption.

Although many groups experience these grand moments when creativity flows and things get done well, the holy grail in business and life is to find ways to sustain these periods of supreme balance. Sustaining innovation is particularly tricky since it flows out of creative disequilibrium.

To achieve sustainable innovation you need to seek persistent disequilibrium. To seek persistent disequilibrium means that one must chase after disruption without succumbing to it, or retreating from it.

A company, institution, or individual must remain perched in an almost-falling state. In this precarious position it is inclined to fall, but continually catches itself and never quite topples. Nor does it anchor itself so that it cannot tip. It sort of skips along within reach of disaster, but uses the power of falling to propel itself forward with grace. A lot of people compare it to surfing; you ride a wave, which is constantly tumbling, and perched on top of this continually disintegrating hill of water, you harness its turbulence into forward motion.

Innovation is hard to institutionalize. It often needs to bend the rules of its own creation. Indeed, by definition innovation means to break away from established patterns, which means that it tends to jump over formulas. In periods of severe flux, such as the transition we are now in between a resource-based economy and a connected-knowledge one, change enters other levels.

Change comes in various wavelengths. There are changes in the game, changes in the rules of the game, and changes in how the rules are changed.

The first level—changes in the game—produces the kind of changes now visible: new winners and losers. New businesses. New heroes. We see the rise of Wal-Marts, and of Nucor steelmaking.

The second level—changes in the rules of the game—produces new kinds of business, new sectors of the economy, new kinds of games. From this type of change comes the Microsofts and Amazon.coms.

The third level of change, which we are now entering, whips up changes in how change happens. Change changes itself. While the new economy provokes change in the first two levels—all those new business and business sectors—its deepest consequence is the way it alters change. Change accelerates itself. It morphs into creative destruction. It induces flux. It disperses into a field effect, so you can't pinpoint causes. It overturns the old ways of change.

Change in technological systems is becoming more biological. This will take a lot of getting used to. Networks actually grow. Evolution can really be imported into machines. Technological immune systems can be used to control computer viruses. This neobiologicalism seeps directly into our new economy. More and more, biological metaphors are useful economic metaphors.

The image of the economy as something alive is powerful. And it is hardly New Age hokum. Adam Smith himself alluded to aliveness with his unseen "hand." Karl Marx often referred to the organic nature of the economy. Even the legendary no-nonsense economist Alfred Marshall wrote in 1948 that "the Mecca of the economist lies in economic biology." Marshall was writing at the peak of the industrial economy. The first stirrings of the coming power of information were just being felt.

Living systems are notoriously hard to model and theorize about, and even more difficult to predict. Until very recently economics has gravitated to an understanding that settled on an equilibrium, primarily because anything more complex was impossible to calculate. Ironically, the very same computer technology, which has roused flux in the economy, is now used to model it. With powerful chips, dynamic, learning, self-feeding theories of the economy can be mapped out.

Both in our understanding of it, and in reality, the network economy is a place that harbors little harmony or stasis. Instead, it is a system that will increasingly demand flux and innovation. The art of judicious change, of the dangerous difference, will be rewarded in full.

Strategies

Skate to the edge of chaos. Pay the price of radical churn: endorse redundancy, inefficiency, and set the neatniks up in arms. If people are not complaining about how chaotic the place is, you've got a problem. It isn't necessary that the whole organization be in chaos (one hopes the accounting department is spared), but that key parts are. The duty may want to be rotated. Realistically, disequilibrium is very difficult to maintain.

Exploit flux instead of outlawing it. The traditional practice of telephony tries to eliminate noise and uncertainty by creating an optimally short and uninterrupted circuit between caller and callee. It assumes a stable route. The internet, on the other hand, counts on chaotic change, and it will overtake the entire phone system soon. It sends messages (including voice) in fragmented bits scattered along redundant routes, and then resends whatever the haphazard process loses to noisy lines. Rather than prohibit errors, network logic assumes errors and learns from the chaotic flux. Find where the flux is, and ride it.

You can't install complexity. Networks are biased against large-scale drastic change. The only way to implement a large new system is to grow it. You can't install it. After the collapse of the Soviet Union, Russia tried to install capitalism, but this complex system couldn't be installed; it had to be grown. The network economy favors assembling large organizations from many smaller ones that keep their autonomy within the large. Networks, too, need to be grown, rather than installed. They need to accumulate over time. To grow a large network, one needs to start with a small network that works, then add more sophisticated nodes and levels to it. Every successful large system was once a successful small system.

Preserve the core, and let the rest flux. In their wonderful bestseller *Built to Last*, authors James Collins and Jerry Porras make a convincing argument that long-lived companies are able to thrive 50 years or more by retaining a very small heart of unchanging values, and then stimulating progress in everything else. At times "everything" includes changing the business the company operates in, migrating, say, from mining to insurance. Outside the core of values, nothing should be exempt from flux. Nothing.

9 RELATIONSHIP TECH
Start with Technology, End with Trust

The central economic imperative of the industrial age was to increase productivity. Every aspect of an industrial firm—from its machines to its organizational structure—was tailored to enhance the efficiency of economic production. But today productivity is a nearly meaningless by-product in the network economy.

The central economic imperative of the network economy is to amplify relationships.

Every aspect of a networked firm—from its hardware to its distributed organization—is created to increase the quantity and quality of economic relationships.

The network is a structure to generate relationships. Networks haul relations the way rivers once hauled freight. When everything is connected to everything else, relationships are rampant. Each variety of connection in a network begets a relationship. Between firms and other firms. Between firms and customers. Between customers and the government. Between customers and other customers. Between employees and other firm's employees. Between customers and machines. Between machines and machines, objects and objects, objects and customers. There is no end to the complexity and subtlety of relationships spawned in a network economy.

Each of these types of relationship has its own specific dynamics and quirks. And each is nurtured by a particular type of technology. The technologies of jelly bean chip and boundless bandwidth are, in the end, relationship technologies. "We need to shift away from the notion of technology managing information and toward the idea of technology as a medium of relationships," writes Michael Schrage in *Shared Minds*, a book about the new technologies of collaboration. Despite the billions of bits that information hardware can process in a second, the only matter of consequence silicon produces are relationships.

Of course reputation and trust have been essential in all economies of the past, so what's new? Only two things:

- With the decreased importance of productivity, relationships and their allies become the main economic event.
- Telecommunications and globalism are intensifying, increasing, and transforming the ordinary state of relationships into an excited state of hyperrelations—over long distances, all the time, all places, all ways. It's not Kansas anymore; it's Oz.

Relationships among more than two people can be structured as hierarchies or as networks. In hierarchies, members are ranked in privilege relative to one another; in networks, members relate as peers—counterparts of similar power and opportunity. In previous ages the most intelligent way to construct a complex organization in the absence of plentiful information was to build a hierarchy. Rank is a clever and workable substitute for ubiquitous real-time information. When information is scarce, follow orders.

When information is plentiful, peers take over.

In fact, as reliable information becomes common, almost nothing can stop peers from taking over. As computers and communications unloose a million bits of information in every dimension, we see peerages form in every dimension. Email and voice mail have brought peerage pressure to corporations. The flattening effect of network technologies and the subsequent turmoil in the organization of business firms is well recognized. But in many ways the emerging peerlike relationship between boss and staff is probably the least interesting and least important of all the relational changes now taking place.

More consequential is the relation between customer and firm, which is yielding to the peer effect. More important still is the relation between firm and firm, which is shifting rapidly to a web of overlapping nets. Still more vital is the lateral relation between customer and customer, which is just beginning to brew. Finally, the elevated relation between customers (rather than citizens) and the rest of society, a relation that is just now being defined, may be the most important of all, as economics elbows its way into every activity. As an example of expanding relationships, consider the traditional relationship between customer and a firm, roles that have been around forever. In the network economy the separation between customers and a firm's employees often vanishes.

When you pump your own gas at the filling station, are you working for the gas station or for yourself? Are all those people waiting in line behind the ATM machine more highly evolved bank customers or just nonpaid bank tellers? When you take a pregnancy test at home, are you a savvy self-helper, or part of the HMO's plan to reduce costs? The answer, of course, is both. When everyone is linked into a web, it's impossible to tell which side you are on.

Web sites and 800 numbers can invite customers into the internal knowledge banks of a company to almost the same degree of "inside" that employees stationed on the other side of the line enjoy. Many technical companies post the same technical information and diagnostic guidelines on their help sites that their own support professionals work from when you call their hotline. You can have someone trained to look up and then read troubleshooting answers for you, or if you are in a hurry, you can try to find it yourself. Who's working for whom?

At the same time the complexity of an employee contract, particularly in high-tech fields, is quickly approaching the complexity of a contract with an outside vendor. Stock options, vestment periods, a thousand insurance and benefit combinations, severance clauses, noncompete agreements, performance goals—each one uniquely negotiated for each person. A highly paid technical employee becomes in essence a permanent consultant. He or she is an outsider on staff.

Outsiders act as employees, employees act as outsiders. New relationships blur the roles of employees and customers to the point of unity. They reveal the customer and company as one.

This close coevolution between users and producers is more than poetry. There is a very real sense in which the owners of the phone network sell nothing at all but the opportunity for customers to have conversations among themselves—conversations which the users themselves create. You could say the phone companies cocreate phone service. This blurring between origin and end spills over into the birth of online services, such as AOL, where most of what is now sold is being created by the customers themselves in the form of postings and chat. It took years for AOL to figure this out; they initially wanted to follow industrial logic and sell downloadable information created at great expense by professionals. But once they realized that the customers acted like employees by making the goods themselves, the online companies started making money.

The net continues to break down the old relationships between producers of goods and consumers of services. Now, producers consume and consumers produce.

In the network economy, producing and consuming fuse into a single verb: prosuming.

"Prosumer" is a term coined by Alvin Toffler in 1970 in his still-prescient book *Future Shock*. (Toffler first found his insights as a futurist while working for the telephone *networks*.) Today prosumers are everywhere, from restaurants where you assemble your own dinner, to medical self-care arenas, where you serve as doctor and patient.

The future of prosumerism can be seen most clearly online, where some of the very best stuff is produced by the people who consume it. In a multiplayer game like Ultima Online, you get a world with a view and some tools and then you're on your own to make it exciting. You invent your own character, develop his or her clothing or uniform, acquire unique powers, and build the surrounding history. All the other thousands of characters you interact with have to be sculpted by other prosumers. The adventures that unfurl are cocreated entirely by the participants. Like a real small town, the joint experience—which is all that is being sold—is produced by those who experience it.

These eager world makers could be viewed as nonpaid content makers; in fact, they will pay you to let them make things. But the same world could also be viewed as full of customers who have been given tools with which they can complete a product to their own picky specifications. They are rolling their own, just as they like. In the new economy-speak, this is known as mass customization.

The premise of mass customization is simple. Technology allows us to target the specifications of a product to a smaller and smaller group of people. First we can make Barbie dolls in the millions. Then with more flexible machinery and computer-generated target marketing we can make ethnic Barbies, in the hundreds of thousands. Then with improved market research and advanced communications we can make subculture Barbies, biker and grunge Barbies in the thousands. Eventually, with the right network technology, we can make the personal Barbie, the Barbie of you. In fact there is a company in Littleton, Colorado, that currently makes the "My Twinn" baby doll to look like the doll's owner. The doll's eye and hair color and hair style are matched to a photo of the child who will own it.

The most interesting aspect of prosuming and mass customization—of this new relationship between the customer and the firm—is that because customers have a hand in the creation of the product they are more likely to be satisfied with the final result. They have taught the firm how to please them, and the firm now has a customer with a much fuller relationship with them than before.

But creating a product for "a niche of one" is only a small part of the transformation of the customer relationship. (Detroit car makers learned long ago to create customized cars, but that was all they learned.) Network technologies such as data mining, smart cards, and recommendation engines are escalating the levels of relationships available to customers.

The drive to relate to the consumer intimately, to the point of encouraging prosuming, can be articulated as a series of progressive goals:

1) to create what the customer wants
2) to remember what the customer wants

3) to anticipate what the customer wants

4) finally, to change what the customer wants

Each of the missions elevates the firm's commitment to the customer and raises the customer's involvement with the firm.

▪ *To create what the customer wants.* Sometimes this will mean simple customization: You want a vacation experience unlike anyone else's. Sometimes this will mean mass customization: You want a pair of jeans that fit your unusual leg shape at the same price as a regular pair of jeans. Sometimes mass customization is not what you want. The huge fashion industry makes its fortune on people's dependable desire for wearing what everyone else is wearing. Sometimes what you want is semicustomized: You read the *New York Times* because everyone else is reading it, but you don't read the sports section or the obits. You want not the *Daily Me*, but the *Daily You and Me*, the publication your 12 closest friends read.

A huge tide of information and trust must flow between users and creators in order to create exactly what the customer wants. The interface technology must be clear and simple for people to convey their desires. The nightmarish logistics of delivery and production must be managed with exactness. The most difficult aspect of this mission may not be the order form but the manufacturing; anything that involves atoms is much harder to customize than first thought. But any solutions surely involve networked technologies.

▪ *To remember what a customer wants.* A majority of the things we do, we do repetitively. We engage in the same tasks every day, or once a week, or every now and then. Things done iteratively have different dynamics from things done once. Little events become important. We bristle at having to remember our password again, or having to recite how we like our coffee one more time, or having to explain again what we don't like about bathing suits. Humans who learn our quirks (and they must be learned) earn our favor. Firms who learn our quirks will also earn our favor.

The technology of tracking and interpreting our whims heightens the relationships between firm and consumer. The firm must expend great effort to remember your preferences, but you also expend effort in teaching them so they can remember. And the remembering must be intelligent. You order the same espresso every day, except when it's cold out, and then you order a latte. The relationship tech has to be robust enough to be taught these distinctions.

Don Peppers and Martha Rogers, authors of the amazingly insightful *Enterprise One to One*, state: "A Learning Relationship between a customer and an enterprise gets smarter and smarter with every individual interaction, defining in ever more detail the customer's own individual needs and tastes. Every time a customer orders her groceries by calling up last week's list and updating it, for instance, she is in effect 'teaching' the service more about the products she buys and the rate at which she consumes them." In reward for the firm's effort at being taught, the firm and the customer develop a committed relationship. Peppers and Rogers continue: "The shopping service will develop a knowledge of this particular customer that is virtually impossible for a competitive shopping service to duplicate, providing an impregnable lock on the customer's loyalty." At the same time, the customer has invested so much in the relationship that the cost of switching to another vendor gets steeper by the day. Peppers and Rogers: "When the florist sends a note reminding you of your mother's birthday, and offers to deliver flowers again this year to the same address and charged against the same credit card you used with the florist last year, what are the chances that you will pick up the phone and try to find a cheaper florist?"

Since a relationship involves two members investing in it, its value increases twice as fast as one's investment.

The cost of switching relationships is high. Leaving, you surrender twice. You give up all that the other has put into the relationship, and you give up your own investment. In other words, the cost of loyalty is low. Thus we see the huge success of frequent flyer and frequent buyer programs, made possible by the coinvestment that airlines and supermarkets put into them. Affiliation cards are another example of the relationship extension; the costs of tracking purchases are so low compared to the value of belonging—for both sides—that it pays to invent other ways to spread the idea. And the phone companies' attempts at "friends of friends" calling circles are likewise clever experiments in exploiting networked relationships.

Smarter relationship technology, or "R-tech" as economist Albert

Bressand calls it, will bind the connections between customers and firms more tightly still. An emerging standard called P3P offers a uniform way to store an individual's profile containing name, address, and so forth as well as preferences, including preferences of what they will reveal. If you shop a lot you will carry a "passport profile" based on the P3P protocol (or one similar) encased in your smart card or online in a browser. You exchange it with the vendor during a commercial transaction. The passport technology will help firms remember you as you teach them how to serve you and earn your favor.

The portability of preferences is a big deal. As the net creeps into yet more aspects of commerce, the ability to track identities and desires across different systems will be key. The Ritz-Carlton Hotel is justifiably proud of its ability to customize rooms for you anywhere in its thirty-one-hotel chain, without having to ask you. Some airlines can do the same. That still leaves a lot of room for success in creating relationships in the network economy as a whole.

■ *To anticipate what a customer wants.* Creating tailored products for people is the first step of R-tech. The second is recalling their preferences intelligently. The third step is anticipating what they'll want even before they articulate it. That's a measure of any great relationship. You can boast you really know someone when you can say, "I know she'll love this book!"

The most elemental form of anticipatory tech extrapolates likes and dislikes from the customer's past usage patterns. But the most powerful forms of R-tech rely on the swarm of other customers and the latent relationships between them to anticipate desires. A great example of this social R-tech was developed by Firefly, a web-based recommendation engine (recently sold to Microsoft). Here's how it works in brief: I tell My-Launch, Firefly's music vendor, my ten favorite music albums. It takes my recommendations and compares them with the top ten recommendations of 500,000 other Firefly members interested in music. Firefly then figures out where in "taste space" I belong. It places me near the few people who like the same albums I do. Despite an overlap of taste with them there will be a few albums my neighbors mentioned that I did not. Firefly will alert me to those albums, and conversely will tell my taste neighbors about the albums I mentioned that they had not.

These are the albums I should try because it anticipates I will like them.

It's remarkable how well this simple system works. I eerily recommended great albums that I liked. There are many refinements to increase its power. I can "teach" the system by grading the results it gave me. Perhaps it recommended Pete Seeger because I named Bob Dylan as a favorite. But say I happen to already know Seeger's work and can't stand him, so I tell it to forget Seeger (and thus Seeger-likes). It's now smarter. I can further locate my space with more precision by rating as many albums as I wish, indicating my love or hate of them. (A strong

Peers in Tastespace

People who share small preferences for particular books or movies in a single "taste space" can use their collaborative sorting to aid them in future purchases.

negative rating is just as useful as a strong positive rating.) Because it is the web, I also have the option of listening to music selections to refresh my memory or evaluate recommended candidates.

The real power of this system lies not in mere recommendation, but in its ability to create relationships among its 3 million registered users. It allows members to link up with their taste-neighbors. All the fans of ambient music, or early Seattle grunge, are encouraged to strike up conversations in "venues," or start mail lists, or simply introduce themselves. Out of this technology is born yet another relationship: self-identity.

Most listeners don't have easily classifiable tastes. They're fans of Nirvana, U2, The Beatles, Joni Mitchell, and Nine Inch Nails. They'll have neighbors in an obscure unnamed space—the Beatles/U2/NineInch-Nails space. Through Firefly, these folks can identify their tastes by the microcommunity of like-minded folks they create for themselves. What Firefly can do with music, it can also do with books. And movies. And web pages. (Firefly recently spun each of these domains out to separate partners.) They are rated in the same way, with equally useful results. But now the combined media space is tremendously potent. Weird subcultures can be detected long before they have a name. Readers of Anne Rice vampire novels who like country and western music and Woody Allen movies suddenly realize they are a group! Self-recognition is the first step toward influence.

Online booksellers such as Amazon.com and Barnes and Noble are using similar R-technology to sell more books, and to make customers smarter shoppers. Amazon derives its collaborative recommendations from customers who have a purchasing behavior similar to yours. Based on what you have bought in the past, and what others have bought in the past, Amazon advises: Dear reader, you should like these titles. And, they are usually right. In fact, their recommendations are so handy that they are Amazon's prime marketing mechanism and their chief source of revenue growth. According to company spokespersons, "significant" numbers of users buy additional books—on impulse—because of the co-recommendations that pop up when you inspect a book.

Evan Schwartz, author of *Webonomics*, goes so far as to suggest that firms such as Amazon should be viewed as primarily selling intangible relationships. "Amazon should not be compared to actual stores selling books. Rather . . . the value that Amazon adds is in the reviews, the recommendations, the advice, the information about new and upcoming releases, the user interface, the community interest around certain subjects. Yes, Amazon will arrange to deliver the book to your door, but you as a customer are really paying them for the information that led to your purchase." When you log on to Amazon you get a relationship generator, one that increasingly knows you better.

The beauty of network logic is that the mechanics of this software does not rely on artificial intelligence, or AI. Rather the collaborative work is done by pooling the teaching that each person would do alone into one distributed base. It's an example of dumb power. Lots of people teaching a dumb program, but all connected together, producing useful intelligence. The strength of the network is built by the slim bits of information that each member is willing to share. Sometimes that's all it takes.

The web is a hotbed of innovations in R-tech. If you had success in a search and are willing for that information to be spread collectively to others, this lateral relationship can improve the search function for everyone. Sometimes called "collaborative filtering" these kinds of social network functions will spread widely within the web itself, as well as within companies and small work groups.

As in other technological evolutions, relationship tech will begin its innovation in the avant garde, then work back to the familiar.

R-tech first appears in the world of the web, but will gradually infiltrate the world of canned goods and sports equipment, as well as TV shows and vacation spots. Eventually it reaches the final stage in the progression of customer relations:

▪ *To change what a customer wants.* The ongoing tango between customer and provider draws them together until their identities disappear at times. This is especially true in frontier arenas, where expertise is usually in short supply. At first this is no authority on what customers want or what providers should deliver—as in these early days of the web and e-commerce. Expertise has to be developed jointly, coevolved. Customers must be trained and educated by the company to teach them what they need, and then the company is trained and educated by the customers. We saw precisely this equation in the pioneer days of online conferencing about a decade ago. When email and chat began, no one knew the difference between great email and okay email, between fabulous chat areas and average chat areas. The best online companies learned all they knew from their first customers. But the customers, too, had little expertise of what to expect and so relied on the visions and vaporware suggested by the companies. Customer and company educated each other on what was possible.

Good products and services are cocreated: The desires of customers grow out of what is possible, and what is possible is made real by companies following new customer desires. Because creation in a network is a cocreation, a prosumptive act, a multifaceted relationship must exist between the cocreators.

Cocreation and prosumption require an information peerage. Information must flow symmetrically to all nodes. In the industrial society, the balance of information inevitably sided with corporations. They had centralized knowledge while the customer had only their own solo experience divorced from that of all but a few friends. The coming network economy has changed that. Each new layer of complexity and technology shifts the action toward the individual.

The intent of networked technology is to make the customer smarter. This may require sharing previously proprietary knowledge with the customer. It may also be as simple as sharing what the company knows about the customer with the customer herself.

R-tech tries to rebalance the traditional asymmetrical flow of information, so that the customer learns as fast as the firm (and so the firm learns as fast as the customer). At first the idea of focusing on "learning customers" instead of the "learning company" seems misplaced. But it is part of the larger shift away from a view of the firm as a standalone unit and toward a view of the firm as an interacting node in a much larger network—a diffuse node made up of customers as well as employees.

Letting the customer learn with help from the firm is not the only way to make the customer smarter. The other way is to reverse the usual flow of information in the market. John Hagel, co-author of *Net Gain*, says, "Instead of helping your firm capture as much information about the customer as you can, you want the customer to capture as much information about themselves as they can." And you want customers to capture as much information about the firms they are dealing with as well. There are several ways on the web to bias information toward the customer. Among the most exciting innovations are new vendors that send a bot around to comparison shop for you. If thirty music retailers online offer the soundtrack to the movie *Titanic* for sale, web sites such as Junglee or Jango will collect the offers from each vendor, and rank them for you. But the vendors are calling the shots; they craft the offer, keep the data of requests, and drive the sale.

By reversing the direction of information flow one can create a "reverse market." In a reverse market (already set by a few web sites), the customer dictates the terms of sale. You say, "I'd like to buy a *Titanic* CD for $10, new." You broadcast your offer into the web, and then the vendors come to you. This works best at first for high-ticket items such as cars, insurance, and mortgages. "I'd like a $120,000 thirty-year mortgage for my house in San Jose. I can pay $1,000 per month. Do I have any takers?" You set the terms, keep the data, and drive the transaction.

Technology, of course, means that much of this negotiation happens in the background via agents and so forth; you don't have to do the haggling yourself. But the R-shift moves the capture of information into the hands of customers from those of the vendors. It makes the customer smarter.

And whoever has the smartest customers wins.

The third way to make the customer smarter is by connecting customers into a collective intelligence.

When personal computers first entered the marketplace in the mid 1970s, user groups sprung up everywhere to assist the perplexed. Anyone could attend a monthly meeting and swap useful tips about how to set up a printer, or get an upgrade program to work. It was all informal, and free, and democratic; those who knew, told; those who didn't know, asked questions and took notes. Each specific computer platform spawned local user groups in major cities. There were user groups for "orphan" equipment such as Amigas, and video game consoles, and of course for Macs and DOS-based PCs. Some user groups grew to have tens of thousands of members and some ran their own free software emporiums and had budgets in the millions of dollars.

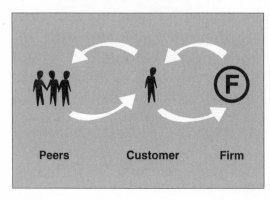

Firms that encourage customers to talk to each other, to form affinity groups and hobby tribes, will breed smarter and more loyal customers while creating smarter products and services.

Peers   Customer   Firm

User groups were seen by the outside world as evidence of the lousy state of the computer industry. Manuals were horrible, interfaces unfriendly. Critics complained that you didn't need to join a user group to get your TV up and running, or to turn your dishwasher on. Yet for many computer wanna-bes, the shared knowledge of a user group was essential in starting the journey into computerdom, or later onto the net and the web.

In reality, user groups were not a sign of failure but a sign of intelligence. They were a means of making the consumer smarter. Some computer companies caught on to this reality early and made regular visits to the bigger user groups to answer questions and hear complaints and pick up suggestions. The user group, although independent and nonprofit, became part of the computer companies' extended self.

Today there are still some 2,000 Mac and PC user groups that offer regular meetings in the United States (and an equal number internationally). The Berkeley Mac User Group still boasts 10,000 members, and *weekly* meetings. Yet most user group action has shifted to the online space. Web sites with attendant conversation areas, FAQ (Frequently Asked Questions) archives, mail lists, and public bulletin boards all keep the distributed exchange of knowledge going.

A user group is a peerage of responsibility. Group members take education into their own hands, and distribute the job of keeping up among themselves. It's long been appreciated that the best and most useful working knowledge about technical gear comes out of user groups. User groups are now a regular feature for avocations such as scuba diving, bicycling, saltwater aquariums, hot-rod cars, or any hobby where technological change seems to outrun understanding.

The most fanatical of user groups can be thought of as "hobby tribes," a phrase coined by science fiction writer David Brin. Hobby tribes are very informed, very connected, very smart customers. They band their enthusiasms together and become the experts. In some smaller niches they become the market, too.

Expertise now resides in fanatical customers. The world's best experts on your product or service don't work for your company. They are your customers, or a hobby tribe.

Companies need user groups almost as much as users need them. User groups are better than advertising when customers are happy, and worse than cancer when they are not. Used properly, aficionados can make or break products.

The network economy has the potential to enable a civilization of aficionados. As customers get smarter, the locus of expertise shifts toward affiliates and home-brew groups, and away from large corporations or the solo academic professional. If you really want to know what works, or where to find it, ask a hobby tribe. And not just in the realm of high-tech knowledge. All knowledge is pooling into aficionados. Because of shared obsessions among horse lovers, there are more horseshoers working today than a hundred years ago, in the age of cowboys. There are more black-smiths making swords and chain mail armor this year than ever worked in the medieval past. A network of aficionados is already here.

The net tends to dismantle authority and shift its allegiance to peer groups. The cultural life in a network economy will not emanate from academia, or the cubicle of corporations, or even primetime media. Rather, it will reside in the small communities of interest known as fans, and 'zines, and subcultures. In *Future Shock* Alvin Toffler sets the stage: "Like a bullet smashing into a pane of glass, industrialism shatters societies, splitting them up into thousands of specialized agencies . . . each subdivided into smaller and still more specialized subunits. A host of subcults spring up; rodeo riders, Black Muslims, motorcyclists, skin-heads, and all the rest." That initial shatter is now several thousands of subcultures. For every obsession in the world, there is now a web site. What industrialization began by shattering, the network economy com-pletes by weaving together and serving with great attention. The web of broken shards is now the big picture.

Information shifts toward the peerage of customers, so does respon-sibility for success. The net demands wiser customers.

The advent of relationship technologies on the net creates a larger role for the customer, and it puts more demands on the consumer, too. None of this enlargement of relationships can happen unless there are vast amounts of trust all around. "The new economy begins with tech-nology and ends with trust," says Alan Weber, founder of the new economy business magazine *Fast Company*.

If you send all your workers home to telecommute, you'll need a whopping lot of trust between you and your workers for that relocation to succeed. If I tell Firefly all the books I read, all the movies I watch, and all the web sites I visit, I will require a high degree of trust from them. If Compaq lets me delve into its expensively compiled knowledge database of known bugs and problems with certain computer parts, it has to trust me.

Trust is a peculiar quality. It can't be bought. It can't be downloaded. It can't be instant—a startling fact in an instant culture. It can only accumulate very slowly, over multiple iterations. But it can disappear in a blink. Alan Weber compares its accretion to a conversation: "The most important work in the new economy is creating conversations. Good conversations are about identity. They reveal who we are to others. And for that reason, they depend on bedrock human qualities: authenticity, character, integrity. In the end, conversation comes down to trust."

A conversation is a pretty good model for understanding what is going on in the network economy. Some conversations are short, abrupt exchanges of minimal data; some are antagonistic, some are periodic, some are continuous, some are long-distance, some are face to face. A back-and-forth exchange starts between two people, and then spills over to several people, and as the conversation becomes multipronged and divergent, it gathers in more and more players. Eventually there are conversations between firms and objects as well as people, as more of the world's inanimate artifacts become connected. Increased animation increases the number or times of interaction, and the frequency of conversation. The more interactions, the more important learning becomes, the more essential relationships become, the more trust becomes a factor. Trust becomes what Weber calls "a business imperative."

But for all the talk of the importance of trust, it only comes at a price. It comes slow and it always comes awkwardly. "Trust can be messy, painful, difficult to achieve, and easy to violate," writes Weber. "Trust is tough because it is always linked to vulnerability, conflict, and ambiguity. For managers steeped in rationalism, hierarchies, rule-based decision making, and authority based on titles, this triad of vulnerability, conflict, and ambiguity threatens a loss of control."

The technologies of relationships will not ease this fear or pain. They can strengthen and diversify relationships and trust, but not make them automatic, easy, or instant. At the forefront in the chore to cultivate trust—as a business imperative—stands the rugged hurdle of privacy. No other issue summarizes the unique opportunities and challenges of the network economy as much as privacy does.

Privacy concerns were once exclusively aimed at Big Brother government, but net residents quickly realized that commercial entities—the little brothers on the net—were more worrisome. James Gleick, a technology correspondent for the *New York Times* put it this way: "Whatever the Government may know about us, it seems that the network itself—that ever-growing complex of connections and computers—will know more. And no matter how much we bristle at the idea, we nevertheless seem to want services that the network can provide only if it knows."

An entire book could be written about the fundamental conversation between what we want to know about others and what we want others and the net itself to know about us. But I will make only a single point about privacy in space of an emerging new economy:

Privacy is a type of conversation. Firms should view privacy not as some inconvenient obsession of customers that must be snuck around but more as a way to cultivate a genuine relationship.

The standard rejoinder by firms to objections from customers for more personal information is, "The more you tell us, the better we can serve you." This is true, but not sufficient. An individual can't comfortably divulge unless there is trust.

Take the trust many people feel in a small town. The interesting thing about a small town is that the old lady who lived across the street from you knew every move you made. She knew who came to visit you and what time they left. From your routine she knew where you went, and why you were late. Two things kept this knowledge from being offensive: 1) When you were out, she kept an eye on your place, and 2) you knew everything about her. You knew who came to visit her and where she went (and while she was gone you kept an eye on her place). More important, you knew that she knew. You were aware that she kept an eye on you, and she knew that you watched her. There was a symmetry to your joint knowledge. There was a type of understanding, of agreement. She wasn't going to rifle through your mailbox, and neither would you peek in hers, but if you had a party and someone passed out on the porch, you could count on the neighborhood knowing about it the next day. And vice versa. The watchers are watched.

One of chief chores in the network economy is to restore the symmetry of knowledge.

For trust to bloom, customers need to know who knows about them, and the full details of what they know. They have to have knowledge about the knower equal to what the knower knows about them. I would be a lot more comfortable with what the credit companies knew about me if I knew with great accuracy what they knew about me, how they know it, and who else they told. And I'd be even more at ease if I derived some compensation for the value they get for knowing about me.

Personally, I'm happy for anyone to track all my activities 24 hours a day, as long as I have a full account of where that information goes and I get paid for it. If I know who the watchers are, and they establish a relationship with me (in cash, discounts, useful information, or superior service, or otherwise), then that symmetry becomes an asset to me and to them.

We see the first inklings of this trust machinery in protocols such as Truste. Truste was founded in 1995 as a nonprofit consortium of web sites and privacy advocates to enhance privacy relationships in the online marketspace. They have developed an information standard also called Truste. The first stage is a system of simple badges posted on the front pages of web sites. These seals alert visitors—before they enter—of the site's privacy policies. The badges declare that either:

- We keep no records of anyone's visit. Or,
- We keep records but only use them ourselves. We know who you are so that when you return we can who show you what's new, or tailor content to your desires, or make purchase transactions easier and simplified. Or,
- We keep records, which we use ourselves, but we also share knowledge with like-minded firms that you may also like.

Those three broad approaches encompass most transactions; but there are as many subvariations as there are sites. (To post the badges or seal, sites must submit to an audit by Truste, which guarantees to the public that a site does adhere to the policies they post.) But the seals are only labels. The real work happens behind the scenes by means of very sophisticated R-tech.

Here is a hypothetical scenario of a visit to a Truste-approved commerce site a couple of years hence. I visit the Gap clothing store online. They notify me that they are a level 2 site; they remember who I am, my clothes size, and what I bought or even inspected last time I visited—but they don't sell that data. In exchange for information about myself, they offer me a 10% discount. Fine with me! Makes life easier. I visit the site of Raven Maps, the best topographical maps in the world. They let me know that my visit with them is on a level 3 basis—they trade my name and interests, but nothing else, with other travel-related sites, which they conveniently list. In exchange they will throw in one free map per purchase. Since the friends of Raven Map look very intriguing, I say yes. I visit CompUSA. They want to know everything about me, and they will sell everything about me, level 3. In exchange, they will lease me a multimedia computer with all the bells and whistles for free. Okay? Ummm, maybe. Then I visit ABC, the streaming video TV place. They declare that they keep no records whatsoever. Whatever shows I watch, only I know. They keep aggregate knowledge, which they use to lure advertisers, but not specifics. A lot of people are attracted to this level 1 total non-survelliance, despite the heavy dose of commercials, and keep coming back.

At the end of the month I get a privacy statement, similar in format to a credit card statement. It lists all the deals and relationships I have agreed to that month and what I can expect. It says I agreed to give the Gap particular personal information, but that information should go no further than them. I gave a pretty detailed personal profile to Raven and the three companies they gave it to show up on my statement. Those three have a one-time use of my data. Raven owes me a map. In the end I gave CompUSA my entire profile. I am owed a computer. The nine vendors they sold my info to also show up; they have unlimited use of my profile and CompUSA web site activities. I'll get junk mail from those nine for a while—but my new computer will be able to filter it all out! In addition, I made a deal with the *New York Times* which lets them keep my reading activities, but nothing else, for a free month's subscription.

Also, my statement shows that American Airlines got my address from ABC, when they claimed level 1. I'll have to have my privacy bot contact them and sort that "mistake" out.

Caller ID, unlisted phone numbers, unlisted email address, individual-free aggregates, personally encrypted medical records, passport profiles, temporary pseudonym badges, digital signatures, biometric passwords, and so on. These are all the technologies we'll be using to sort out the messy business of creating relationships and trust in a network economy.

If only we knew precisely what relationships were. Industrial productivity was easy to measure. One could ascertain a clear numerical answer. Relationships, on the other hand, are indefinite, fuzzy, imprecise, complex, innumerate, slippery, multifaceted. Much like the net itself.

As we create technologies of relationships we keep running into the soft notions of reputation, privacy, loyalty, and trust. Unlike bit or baud, there's no good definition of what these concepts mean exactly, though we have some general ideas. Yet we are busy engineering a network world to transmit and amplify reputations and loyalty and trust. The hottest, hippest frontiers on the net today are the places where these technologies are being developed.

The network economy is founded on technology, but can only be built on relationships. It starts with chips and ends with trust.

Ultimately the worth of a technology is judged by how well it facilitates an increase in relational activity. VR pioneer Jaron Lanier has proposed the Connection Test: Does a technology in question connect people together? By his evaluation telephones are good technology, while TV is not. Birth control pills are, while nuclear power is not.

By this measure, network technology is a great deal. It has the potential to link together all kinds of sentient beings in every imaginable way, and more. The imperative of the network economy is to maximize the unique needs and talents of individual beings by means of their relationships with many others.

That means not being connected at times. Silence is often an appropriate response in a conversation. Privacy is often advantageous in a networked world. The dimensions of relationship extend into not knowing as well as into the known. It is one of many mysteries in the human condition that will be wired into the technologies of the network economy.

Strategies

Make customers as smart as you are. For every effort a firm makes in educating itself about the customer, it should expend an equal effort in educating the customer. It's a tough job being a consumer these days. Any help will be rewarded by loyalty. If you don't educate your customer, someone else will—most likely someone not even a competitor. Almost any technology that is used to market to customers, such as data mining, or one-to-one techniques, can be flipped around to provide intelligence to the customer. No one is eager for a core dump, but if you can remember my trouser size, or suggest a movie that all my friends loved, or sort out my insurance needs, then you are making me smarter. The rule is simple: Whoever has the smartest customers wins.

Connect customers to customers. Nothing is as scary to many corporations as the idea of sponsoring dens in which customers can talk to one another. Especially if it is an effective place of communication. Like the web. "You mean," they ask in wonder, "we should pay a million dollars to develop a web site where customers can swap rumors and make a lot of noise? Where complaints will get passed around and the flames of discontent fanned?" Yes, that's right. Often that's what will happen. "Why should we pay our customers to harass us," they ask, "when they will do that on their own?" Because there is no more powerful force in the network economy than a league of connected customers. They will teach you faster than you could learn any other way. They will be your smartest customers, and, to repeat, whoever has the smartest customers wins.

Just recently E-trade, the pioneering online stock broker, took the bold step of setting up an online chat area for its customers. We'll see more smart companies do this. Whatever tools you develop that will aid the creation of relationships *between your customers* will strengthen the relationship of your customers to you. This effort can also be thought of as Feeding the Web First.

All things being equal, choose technology that connects. Technology tradeoffs are made daily. A device or method cannot be the fastest,

cheapest, more reliable, most universal, and smallest all at once. To excel, a tech has to favor some dimensions over others. Now add to that list,
most connected. This aspect of technology has increasing importance, at
times overshadowing such standbys as speed and price. If you are in
doubt about what technology to purchase, get the stuff that will connect
the most widely, the most often, and in the most ways. Avoid anything
that resembles an island, no matter how well endowed that island is.

Imagine your customers as employees. It is not a cheap trick to get
the customer to do what employees used to do. It's a way to make a better
world! I believe that everyone would make their own automobile if it was
easy and painless. It's not. But customers at least want to be involved at
some level in the creation of what they use—particularly complex things
they use often. They can superficially be involved by visiting a factory
and watching their car being made. Or they can conveniently order a
customized list of options. Or, through network technology, they can be
brought into the process at various points. Perhaps they send the car
through the line, much as one follows a package through FedEx. Smart
companies have finally figured out that the most accurate way to get customer information, such as a simple address, without error, is to have the
customer type it themselves right from the first. The trick will be finding
where the limits of involvement are. Customers are a lot harder to get rid
of than employees! Managing intimate customers requires more grace
and skill than managing staff. But these extended relationships are more
powerful as well.

The final destiny for the future of the company often seems to be the
"virtual corporation"—the corporation as a small nexus with essential
functions outsourced to subcontractors. But there is an alternative vision
of an ultimate destination—the company that is only staffed by customers. No firm will ever reach that extreme, but the trajectory that leads
in that direction is the right one, and any step taken to shift the balance
toward relying on the relationships with customers will prove to be an
advantage.

10 OPPORTUNITIES BEFORE EFFICIENCIES
Don't Solve Problems; Seek Opportunities

Until Charles Darwin's discovery of evolution, life was surveyed in the present tense. Animals were probed to see how their innards worked, plants dissected for useful magical potions, the creatures of the sea investigated for their strange lifestyles. Biology was about how living organisms thrived day to day.

Darwin forever transformed our understanding of life by insisting that life didn't make sense without the framework of its billion-year evolution. Darwin proved that even if all we wanted to know was how to cure dysentery in pigs, or how best to fertilize corn, or where to look for lobsters, we had to keep in mind the slow, but commanding dynamics of life's evolution over the very long term.

Until recently, economics was about how businesses thrived year to year, and what kind of governmental policy to institute in the next quarter. The dynamics of long-term growth are quite remote from the issues of whether the money supply should be tightened this year. The study of economics has no Darwin yet, but it is increasingly clear that the behavior of everyday markets cannot be truly understood without keeping in mind the slow, but commanding dynamics of long-term economic growth.

Over the long run, the world's economy has grown, on average, a fractional percent per year. During the last couple of centuries it averaged about 1% per year, reaching about 2% annually this century, when the bulk of what we see on earth today was built. That means that each year, on average, the economic system produces 2% more stuff than was produced in the previous 12 months. Beneath the frantic ups and downs of daily commerce, a persistent, invisible swell pushes the entire econosphere forward, slowly thickening the surface of the earth with more things, more interactions, and more opportunities. And that tide is accelerating, expanding a little faster each year.

At the genesis of civilization, the earth was mostly Darwin's realm—all biosphere, no economy. Today the econosphere is huge beyond comprehension. If we add up the total replacement costs of all the roads in every country in the world, all the railways, vehicles, telephone lines, power plants, schools, houses, airports, bridges, shopping centers (and everything inside them), factories, docks, harbors—if we add up all the gizmos and things humans have made all over the planet, and calculate how much it is all worth, as it if were owned by a company, we come up with a huge amount of wealth accumulated over centuries by this slow growth. In 1998 dollars, the global infrastructure is worth approximately 4 quadrillion dollars. That's a 4 with 15 zeros. That's a lot of pennies from nothing.

What is the origin of this wealth? Ten thousand years ago there was almost none. Now there is 4 quadrillion dollars worth. Where did all of it come from? And how? The expenditure of energy needed to create this fluorescence is not sufficient to explain it since animals expend vast quantities of energy without the same result. Something else is at work. "Humans on average build a bit more than they destroy, and create a bit more than they use up," writes economist Julian Simon. That's about right, but what enables humans, on average, to ratchet up such significant accumulations?

The ratchet is the Great Asymmetry, says evolutionist Steven Jay Gould. This is the remarkable ability of evolution to create a bit more, on average, than it destroys. Against the great drain of entropy, life ratchets up irreversible gains. The Great Asymmetry is rooted in webs, in tightly interlinked entities, in self-reinforcing feedback, in coevolution, and in the many loops of increasing returns that fill an ecosystem. Because every new species in life cocreates a niche for yet other new species to occupy, because every additional organism presents a chance for other organisms to live upon it, the cumulative total multiplies up faster than the inputs add up; thus the perennial one-way surplus of opportunities.

We call the Great Asymmetry in human affairs "the economy." It too is packed with networks of webs that multiply outputs faster than inputs.

Therefore, on average, it fills up faster than it leaks. Over the long run, this slight bias in favor of creation can yield a world worth 4 quadrillion dollars.

It is not money the Great Asymmetry accrues, nor energy, nor stuff. The origin of economic wealth begins in opportunities.

The first object made by human hands opened an opportunity for someone else to imagine alternative uses or alternative designs for that object. If those new designs or variations were manifested, then these objects would create further opportunities for new uses and designs. One actualized artifact yielded two or more opportunities for improvement. Two improvements yielded two new opportunities each—now there were four possibilities. Four yielded eight. Thus over time the number of opportunities were compounded. Like the doubling of the lily leaf, one tiny bloom can expand to cover the earth in relatively few generations.

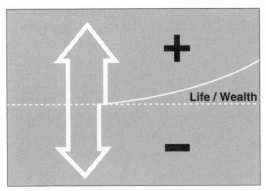

Both life and wealth expand by compounding increase, which gives them an eternal slight advantage over death and loss, so that over time there is constant growth.

Life / Wealth

Perhaps the most potent physical force on earth is the power of compounded results, whether that is compounded interest, compounded growth, compounded life, or compounded opportunities. The inputs of energy and human time into the economy can only be supplied in an additive function, bit by bit, but over time the output is multiplied to compound upon itself, yielding astounding accumulations.

A steady stream of human attention and thought is applied to inventing new tools, devising new amusements, and creating new wants. But no matter how small and inconsequential, each innovation is a platform for yet other innovations to launch from.

It is this expanding space of opportunities that creates an ongoing economy. It is this boundless open-ended arena for innovations that spurs wealth creation. Like a chain reaction, one well-placed innovation can trigger dozens, if not hundreds, of innovation offspring down the line.

Consider, for example, email. Email is a recent invention that has ignited a frenzy of innovation and opportunity. Each tiny bit of email ingenuity begets several other bits of ingenuity, and they each in turn beget others, and so on compoundfinitum. Unlike a piece of junk mail, an email advertisement costs exactly the same to send to one person or one million people—assuming you have a million addresses. Where does one get a million addresses? People innocently post their addresses all over the net—at the bottom of their home page, or in a posting on a news group, or in a link off an article. These postings suggested an open opportunity to programmers. One of them came up with the idea of a scavenger bot. (A bot, short for robot, is a small bit of code.) A scavenger bot roams the net looking for any phrase containing the email @ sign, assumes it is an address, pockets it, and then compiles lists of these addresses that are sold for $20 per thousand to spammers—the folks who mail unsolicited ads (junk mail) to huge numbers of recipients.

The birth of scavenger bots suddenly created niches for anti-spam bots. Companies that sell internet access seed the net with decoy phony email addresses so that when the addresses are picked up by scavenger bots and used by the spammers, the internet provider will get mail they can track to find out where the spam is coming from. Then the provider blocks the spam from that source for all their customers, which keeps everyone happy and loyal.

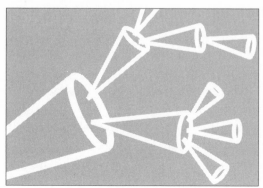

Each new invention creates a space from which several more inventions can be created. And from each of those new innovations comes yet more spaces of opportunity.

Naturally, that innovation creates opportunity for yet more innovation. Creative spammers devised technology that allows them to fake their source address; they hijack someone else's legitimate address to mail spam from and then flee after using it.

Every move generates two countermoves. Every innovation creates an opportunity for two other innovations to succeed by it.

Every opportunity seized launches at least two new opportunities.

The entire web is an opportunity dynamo. More than 320 million web pages have been created in the first five years of the web's existence. Each day 1.5 million new pages of all types are added. The number of web sites—now at 1 million—is doubling every 8 months. (Think lily pond!) A single opportunity seized in 1989 by a bored researcher began this entrepreneurial bloom. It is not the lily leaf that is expanding now, but the lily pond itself.

The number of opportunities, like the number of ideas, are limitless. Both are created combinatorially in the way words are. You can combine and recombine the same 26 letters to write an infinite number of books. The more components you begin with, the faster the total possible combinations ramp up to astronomical numbers. Paul Romer, an economist working on the nature of economic growth, points out that the number of possible arrangements of bits on a CD is about $10^{billion}$. Each arrangement would be a unique piece of software or music. But this number is so huge there aren't enough atoms in the universe to physically make that many CDs, even subtracting all the duds that are just random noise.

We can rearrange more than just bits. Think of the mineral iron oxide, suggests Romer. It's rust. More than 10,000 years ago our ancestors used iron oxide as a pigment to make art on cave walls. Now, by rearranging those same atoms into a precisely thin iron oxide film on plastic we get a floppy disk, which can hold a reproduction of the same cave paintings, and all the possible permutations of it wrought by Photoshop. We have amplified the possibilities a millionfold.

The power of combinatorial explosions—which is what you get with ideas and opportunities—means, says Romer, "There's essentially no scarcity to deal with." Because the more you use opportunities, the less scarce they get.

Everything we know about the structure of the network economy suggests that it will bolster this efflorescence of opportunities, for the following reasons:

- Every opportunity inhabits a connection. As we connect up more and more of the world into nodes on a network, we make available billions more components in the great combinatorial game. The number of possibilities explodes.
- Networks speed the transmission of opportunities seized and innovations created, which are disseminated to all parts of the network and the planet, inviting more opportunities to build upon them.

Technology is no panacea. It will never solve the ills or injustices of society. Technology can do only one thing for us—but it is an astonishing thing: Technology brings us an increase in opportunities.

Long before Beethoven sat before a piano, someone with twice his musical talents was born into a world that lacked keyboards or orchestras. We'll never hear his music because technology and knowledge had not yet uncovered those opportunities. Centuries later the fulfilled opportunity of musical technology gave Beethoven the opportunity to be great. How fortunate we are that oil paints had been invented by the time Van Gogh was ready, or that George Lucas could use film and computers. Somewhere on Earth today are young geniuses waiting for a technology that will perfectly match their gifts. If we are lucky, they'll live long enough for our knowledge and technology to make the opportunity they need.

Oil paint, keyboard, opera, pen—all these opportunities remain. But in addition we have added film, metal work, skyscrapers, hypertext, and holograms as but a few of the new opportunities for artistic expression. Each year we add more opportunities of every stripe. Ways to see. Methods for thinking. Means of amusing. Paths to health. Routes to understanding.

The Great Asymmetry of economic life ceaselessly amasses new opportunities while relinquishing few old ones. The one-way journey is toward more and more possibilities, pointing in more and more directions, opening more and more new territories.

"A few decades from now there will be ten billion people on the planet, and sophisticated computers will be cheaper than transistor radios," writes science fiction writer David Brin in his manifesto *The*

Transparent Society. "If this combination does not lead to war and chaos, then it will surely result in a world where countless men and women swarm the dataways in search of something special to do—some pursuit outside the normal range, to make each one feel just a little bit extraordinary. Through the internet, we may be seeing the start of a great exploration aimed outward in every conceivable direction of interest or curiosity. An expedition to the limits of what we are, and what we might become."

As the transmission of knowledge accelerates, as more possibilities are manufactured, the unabated push of incremental growth also speeds up. In the long run, creating and seizing opportunities is what drives the economy. A better benchmark than productivity would be to measure the number of possibilities generated by a company or innovation and use the total to evaluate progress.

In the short run, though, problems must be solved. Businesses are taught that they are in the business of solving problems. Put your finger on a customer's dissatisfaction, the MBAs say, and then deliver a solution. This bit of hoary advice inspires business to seek out problems. Problems, however, are entities that don't work. They are usually situations where the goal is clear but the execution falls short. As in, "We have a reliability problem," or "Customers complain about out late delivery." In the words of Peter Drucker, "Don't solve problems." George Gilder distills the essence further: "When you are solving problems, you are feeding your failures, starving your successes, and achieving costly mediocrity. In a competitive global arena, costly mediocrity goes out of business."

"Don't solve problems; pursue opportunities."

Seeking opportunities is no longer wisdom relevant only to the long cycles of economic progress. As the economy speeds up, so that an "internet year" seems to pass in one month, the principles of long-term growth begin to govern the day-to-day economy. The dynamics of growth become the dynamics of short-term competitive advantage.

In both the short and long term, our ability to solve social and economic problems will be limited primarily to our lack of imagination in seizing opportunities, rather than trying to optimize solutions.

There is more to be gained by producing more opportunities than by optimizing existing ones.

Optimization and efficiency die hard. In the past, better tools made our work more efficient. So economists reasonably expected that the coming information age would be awash in superior productivity. That's what better tools gave us in the past. But, surprisingly, the technology of computers and networks have not yet led to measurable increases in productivity.

Increasing efficiency brought us our modern economy. By producing more output per labor input, we had more goods at cheaper prices. That raised living standards. The productivity factor is so fundamental to economic growth that it became the central economic measurement tracked and perfected by governments. As economist Paul Krugman once said, "Productivity isn't everything, but in the long run it is almost everything."

Productivity, however, is exactly the wrong thing to care about in the new economy.

To measure efficiency you need a uniform output. But uniform output is becoming rarer in an economy that emphasizes smaller production runs, total customization, personalized "feelgoods" and creative innovation. Less and less is uniform.

And machines have taken over the uniform. They love tedious and measurable work. Constant upgrades enable them to churn out more per hour. So the only ones who should worry about their own productivity are those made of ball bearings and rubber hoses. And, in fact, the one area of the current economy that does show a rise in productivity has been the U.S. and Japanese manufacturing sectors, which have seen an approximately 3% to 5% annual increase throughout the 1980s and into the 1990s. This is exactly where you want to find productivity. Each worker, by the supervising machinery and tools, produces more rivets, more batteries, more shoes, and more items per person-hour. Efficiencies are for robots.

Opportunities, on the other hand, are for humans. Opportunities demand flexibility, exploration, guesswork, curiosity, and many other qualities humans excel at. By its recursive nature, a network breeds opportunities, and incidentally, jobs for humans.

Where humans are most actively engaged with their imaginations, we don't see productivity gains—and why would we? Is a Hollywood movie company that produces longer movies per dollar more productive than one that produces shorter movies? Yet an increasingly greater percentage of work takes place in the information, entertainment, and communication industries where the "volume" of output is somewhat meaningless.

The problem with trying to measure productivity is that it measures only how well people can do the wrong jobs. Any job that can be measured for productivity probably should be eliminated from the list of jobs that people do.

The task for each worker in the industrial age was to discover how to do his job better: that's productivity. Frederick Taylor revolutionized industry by using his scientific method to optimize mechanical work. But in the network economy, where machines do most of the inhumane work of manufacturing, the question for each worker is not "How do I do this job right?" but "What is the right job to do?"

Answering this question is, of course, extremely hard to do. It's called an executive function. In the past, only the top 10% of the workforce was expected to make such decisions. Now, everyone, not just executives, must decide what is the right next thing to do.

In the coming era, doing the exactly right next thing is far more fruitful than doing the same thing better.

But how can one easily measure this vital sense of exploration and discovery? It will be invisible if you measure productivity. But in the absence of alternative measures, productivity has become a bugaboo. It continues to obsess economists because there is little else they know how to measure consistently.

As bureaucrats continue to measure productivity, they find no substantial increase in recent decades. This despite $700 billion invested into computer technology worldwide each year. Millions of people and companies worldwide purchase computer technology because it increases the quality of their work, but in the aggregate there is no record of their benefits in the traditional measurements. This unexpected finding is called the productivity paradox. As Nobel laureate Robert Solow once quipped, "Computers can be found everywhere except in economic statistics."

There is no doubt that many past purchases of computer systems were bungled, mismanaged, and squandered. Last year 8,000 mainframe computers—computers with the power of a Unix box and the price of a large building—were sold to customers imprisoned by legacy systems. IBM alone sold $5 billion worth of mainframes in 1997. Those billions don't help the efficiency ratings. The year 2000 fiasco is a world-scale screwup that also saps the payoff from information technology. But according to economic historian Paul David, it took the smokestack economy 40 years to figure out how to reconfigure their factories to take advantage of the electric motor, invented in 1881; for the first decade of the changeover productivity actually decreased. David likes to quip that "In 1900 contemporaries might well have said that the electric dynamos were to be seen 'everywhere but in the economic statistics.' " And the switch to electric motors was simple compared to the changes required by network technology.

At this point we are still in just the third decade of the age of the microprocessor. Productivity will rebound. In a few years it will "suddenly" show up in elevated percentages. But contrary to Krugman's assertion, in the long run productivity is almost nothing. Not because productivity increases won't happen; they will. But because, like the universal learning curve that brings costs plunging down, increased productivity is a rote process.

The learning curve of inverted prices was first observed by T. P. Wright, a legendary engineer who built airplanes after the First World War. Wright kept records of the numbers of hours it took to assemble each plane and calculated that the time dropped as the total number of units completed increased. The more experience assemblers had, the greater their productivity. At first this was thought to be relevant only to airplanes, but in the 1970s engineers at Texas Instruments began applying the rule to semiconductors. Since then the increase of productivity with experience is seen everywhere. According to Michael Rothschild, author of *Bionomics*, "Data proving learning-curve cost declines have been published for steel, soft contact lenses, life insurance policies, automobiles, jet engine maintenance, bottle caps, refrigerators, gasoline refining, room air conditioners, TV picture tubes, aluminum, optical fibers, vacuum cleaners, motorcycles, steam turbine generators, ethyl alcohol, beer, facial tissues, transistors, disposable diapers, gas ranges, float glass, long distance telephone calls, knit fabric lawn mowers, air travel, crude oil production, typesetting, factory maintenance, and hydroelectric power."

As the law of increasing productivity per experience was seen to be universal, another key observation was made: The learning didn't have to take place within one company. The experience curve could be seen across whole industries. Easy, constant communication spreads experience throughout a network, enabling everyone's production to contribute to the learning. Rather than have five companies each producing 10,000 units, network technologies allow the five to be virtually grouped so that in effect there is one company producing 50,000 units, and everyone shares the benefits of experience. Since there is a 20% drop in cost for every doubling of experience, this network effect adds up. Advances in network communications, standard protocols for the transmission of technical data, and the informal, ad hoc communities of technicians all spread this whirlwind of experience, and ensures the routine rise of productivity.

Analyst Andrew Kessler of Velocity Capital Management compares the plummeting of prices due to the universal learning curve to a low pressure front in the economy. Just as a meterological low pressure system sucks in weather from the rest of the country, the low pressure point generated by sinking prices sucks in investments and entrepreneurial zeal to create opportunities.

Opportunities and productivity work hand in hand much like the two-step process of variation and death in natural selection. The primary role that productivity plays in the network economy is to disperse technologies. A technical advance cannot leverage future opportunities if it is hoarded by a few. Increased productivity lowers the cost of acquisition of knowledge, techniques, or artifacts, allowing more people to have them. When transistors were expensive they were rare, and thus the opportunities built upon them were rare. As the productivity curve kicked in, transistors eventually became so cheap and omnipresent that anyone could explore their opportunities. When ball bearings were dear, opportunities sired by them were dear. As communication becomes everywhere dirt cheap and ubiquitous, the opportunities it kindles will likewise become unlimited.

The network economy is destined to be a fount of routine productivity. Technical experience can be shared quickly, increasing efficiencies in automation. The routine productivity of machines, however, is not what humans want. Instead, what the network economy demands from us is something that looks suspiciously like waste.

Wasting time and inefficiencies are the way to discovery. When Condé Nast's editorial director Alexander Liberman was challenged on his inefficiencies in producing world-class magazines such *The New Yorker, Vanity Fair*, and *Architectural Digest*, he said it best: "I believe in waste. Waste is very important in creativity." Science fiction ace William Gibson declared the web to be the world's largest waste of time. But this inefficiency was, Gibson further noted, its main attraction and blessing, too. It was the source of art, new models, new ideas, subcultures, and a lot more. In a network economy, innovations must first be seeded into the inefficiencies of gift economy to later sprout in efficiencies of the commerce.

Before the World Wide Web there was Dialog. Dialog was pretty futuristic. In the 1970s and '80s it was the closest thing to an electronic library there was, containing the world's scientific, scholarly, and journalistic texts. The only problem was its price, $1 per minute. You could spend a lot of money looking things up. At those prices only serious questions were asked. There was no fooling around, no making frivolous queries—like looking up your name. Waste was discouraged. Since searching was sold as a scarcity, there was little way to master the medium, or to create anything novel.

It takes 56 hours of wasting time on the web—clicking aimlessly through dumb web sites, trying stuff, and making tons of mistakes and silly requests—before you master its search process. The web encourages inefficiency. It is all about creating opportunities and ignoring problems. Therefore it has hatched more originality in a few weeks than the efficiency-oriented Dialog system has in its lifetime, that is, if Dialog has ever hatched anything novel at all.

The Web is being run by 20-year-olds because they can afford to waste the 56 hours it takes to become proficient explorers. While 45-year-old boomers can't take a vacation without thinking how they'll justify the trip as being productive in some sense, the young can follow hunches and create seemingly mindless novelties on the web without worrying about whether they are being efficient. Out of these inefficient tinkerings will come the future.

Faster than the economy can produce what we want, we are exploring in every direction, following every idle curiosity, and inventing more wants to satisfy. Like everything else in a network, our wants are compounding exponentially.

Although at some fundamental level our wants connect to our psyches, and each desire can be traced to some primeval urge, technology creates ever new opportunities for those desires to find outlets and form. Some deep-rooted human desires found expression only when the right technology came along. Think of the ancient urge to fly, for instance.

KLM, the official Dutch airline, sells a million dollars worth of tickets per year to people who fly trips to nowhere. Customers board the plane on whatever international flight KLM has extra seats on, and make an immediate round-trip flight, returning without leaving the airport at the other end. The flight is like a high-tech cruise, where duty-free shopping and simply flying in a 737 at a steep discount is the attraction. Where did this want come from? It was created by technology.

Finance writer Paul Pilzer notes perceptively that "When a merchant sells a consumer a new Sony Walkman for $50, he is in fact creating far more demand than he is satisfying—in this case a continuing and potentially unlimited need for tape cassettes and batteries." Technology creates our needs faster than it satisfies them.

Needs are neither fixed nor absolute. Instead they are fluid and reflexive. The father of virtual reality, Jaron Lanier, claims that his passion for inventing VR systems came from a long-frustrated urge to play "air guitar"—to be able to wave his arms and have music emanate from his motions. Anyone with access to a VR arcade can now have that urge satisfied, but it is a want that most people would have never recognized until they immersed themselves into virtual reality gear. It was certainly not a primary want that Plato would have listed.

At one time a useful distinction was made in economics between "primary" needs such as food and clothing, and all other wants and preferences, which were termed "luxuries." Advertising is undoubtedly guilty, as critics charge, of creating desires. At first these manufactured desires were for luxuries. But the reach of technology is deep. Sophisticated media technology first creates desires for luxuries; then technology transforms those luxuries into primary necessities.

A dry room with running water, electric lights, a color TV, and a toilet are considered so elementary and primary today that we outfit jail cells with this minimum technology. Yet three generations ago, this technology would have been officially classified as outright luxurious, if not frivolous. In the government's eyes 93% of Americans officially classified as living in poverty have a color TV, and 60% have a VCR and a microwave. Poverty is not what it used to be. Technological knowledge constantly ups the ante. Most Americans today would find living without a refrigerator and telephone to be primitive, indeed. These items were luxuries only 60 years ago. At this point an automobile of one's own is considered a primary survival need of any adult.

"Need" is a loaded word. The key point in economic terms is that each actualization of a desire—that is, new each service or product—forms a platform from which other possible activities can be imagined and desired. Once technology satisfies the opportunity to fly, for instance, flying produces new desires: to eat while flying, to fly by oneself to work each day, to fly faster than sound, to fly to the moon, to watch TV while flying. Once technology satisfies the desire to watch TV while flying, our insatiable imagination hungers to be able to watch a video *of our own choosing*, and to not see what others watch. That dream, too, can be actualized by technical knowledge. Each actualization of an idea supplies room for more technology, and each new technology supplies room for more ideas. They feed on each other, rounding faster and faster.

This ever-extending loop whereby technology generates demand, and then supplies the technology to meet those demands is the origin of progress. But it is only now being viewed as such. In classical economics—based on the workings of the brick and smokestack—technology was a leftover. To explain economic growth, economists tallied up the effects of the traditional economic ingredients such as labor, capital, and inventory. This aggregate became the equation of growth. Whatever growth was not explained by those was attributed to a residual category: technology. Technology was thus defined as outside the economic engine. It was also assumed to be a fixed quantity—something that didn't really change itself. Then in 1957 Robert Solow, an economist working at MIT, calculated that technology is responsible for about 80% of growth.

We see now, particularly with the advent of the network economy, that technology is not the residual, but the dynamo. In the new order, technology is the Prime Mover.

Our minds will at first be bound by old rules of economic growth and productivity. Listening to the technology can loose them. Technology says, rank opportunities before efficiencies. For any individual, organization, or country the key decision is not how to raise productivity by doing the same better, but how to negotiate among the explosion of opportunities, and choose right things to do.

The wonderful news about the network economy is that it plays right into human strengths. Repetition, sequels, copies, and automation all tend toward the free and efficient, while the innovative, original, and imaginative—none of which results in efficiency—soar in value.

Strategies

Why can't a machine do this? If there is pressure to increase the productivity of human workers, the serious question to ask is, why can't a machine do this? The fact that a task is routine enough to be measured suggests that it is routine enough to go to the robots. In my opinion, many of the jobs that are being fought over by unions today are jobs that will be outlawed within several generations as inhumane.

Scout for upside surprises. The qualities needed to succeed in the network economy can be reduced to this: a facility for charging into the unknown. Disaster lurks everywhere, but so do unexpected bonanzas. But the Great Asymmetry ensures that the upside potential outweighs the downside, even though nine out of ten tries will fail. Upside benefits tend to cluster. When there are two, there will be more. A typical upside surprise is an innovation that satisfies three wants at once, and generates five new ones, too.

Maximize the opportunity cascade. One opportunity triggers another. And then another. That's a rifle-shot opportunity burst. But if one opportunity triggers ten others and those ten others after, it's an explosion that cascades wide and fast. Some seized opportunities burst completely laterally, multiplying to the hundreds of thousands in the first generation—and then dry up immediately. Think of the pet rock. Sure, it sold in the millions, but then what? There was no opportunity cascade. The way to determine the likelihood of a cascade is to explore the question: How many other technologies or businesses can be started by others based on this opportunity?

A Thousand Points of Wealth

The network economy will unleash opportunities on a scale never seen before on Earth. But the network economy is not utopia. It is a unique phase of economic development much like adolescence—a thrilling, disorienting, and never-to-be repeated time. The planet can progress only once through the stage when it is first completely wrapped by networks of thought and interaction. We are now at that moment when a cloak of glass fibers and a halo of satellites are closing themselves around the globe to bring forth a seamless economic culture.

This new global economic culture is characterized by decentralized ownership and equity, by pools of knowledge instead of pools of capital, by an emphasis on an open society, and, most important, by a widespread reliance on economic values as the basis for making decisions in all walks of life.

The sources of capital, which in the industrial age were once consolidated in a few banks and individual "capitalists," are now fragmenting into millions of networked bank accounts, mutual funds, and private investments throughout society. Elite, centralized banks used to have a monopoly on capital—the engine of capitalism. Bankers loaned their assets as debt, and from this debt, industry rose. But with increased knowledge and communication, investors realized that partnerships—or investments where the investor shares risk—yield significantly more wealth in the long run. Technology has accelerated the migration from making loans to making investments. The ease of computerized accounting allows almost anyone with as little as $100 to plug into the network of equity. Despite the rise of a few gigantic global banks, increasing amounts of the wealth are now held in equity, and not in debt. Today, for instance, 28% of U.S. household assets are kept in equities—more than is kept in banks—and 44% of U.S. households own stock.

Networks promote this equity culture. The ownership of organizations is distributed and decentralized into a thousand points. The transactional costs of owning a tiny share of someone's else's dreams and ambitions continues to drop so that it becomes feasible to possess, directly and indirectly, small parts of many companies. When you invest in a mutual fund, you invest in hundreds of thousands of other people's work. You use the wealth that your own ambition has generated to seed the generation of prosperity by others. You may own only some minuscule portion of an enterprise, but you can easily own parts of many firms, and each firm is owned by millions of individuals. This is network equity.

Out of this distributed ownership a portrait of a network emerges. Millions of lines of investment crisscross the landscape. A few individuals own a lot, but the majority of nodes are dispersed into small bank accounts in small towns. The bulk of stocks in the United States are controlled by the pension funds of ordinary citizens—by millions of individuals in the aggregate. The workers of America really do collectively own the means of production.

This network equity is made possible by the same network technology—shrinking chips and expanding communications—that creates wealth in the first place. The tracking, accounting, and transmission of each person's wealth and slivers of ownership can happen only because computation and telecommunication have reduced the cost of a transaction to insignificance, Today there are 7,000 mutual funds—7,000 ways to divvy up the equity of wealth creation. And there are a similar number of publicly traded companies that have, in effect, divvied up their wealth to many owners.

There are several trends in this emerging equity culture, each one amplified by pervasive network technology.

First, the spread of ownership is becoming global, just as the economy itself is. In the last few years, Europe has suddenly sent a mind-boggling infusion of money into the stock markets. Europeans discovered equity culture and overnight invested hundreds of billions of dollars of their old wealth into the network of ownership. At the same time, hungry investors are pouring billions into the coffers of Asian and Latin

American "emerging markets." Today, almost any investor in mutual funds, whether he knows it or not, has a stake in a company operating in a nation outside his own.

Second, as the ease and price of transactions drop, the spread of ownership becomes fine-grained and ever wider. Smaller and smaller investments into more and more varieties of endeavors are possible. Several banks are following the lead of the Grameen Bank of Bangladesh and offering microloans. These loans amount to U.S. $100 or less, and are made to third-worlders who use the money to buy a cow, purchase some yarn, or begin some other microentrepreneurial dream. The payback rate is around 95%, making these almost as risk-free as bonds. As one banking report says, "Lending to poor people in the shanty towns of La Paz may be safer for banks than lending to the government of Bolivia itself." Large commercial banks have noticed the U.S. $7 billion already lent to 13 million people around the world, and are bringing "microfinance" into the mainstream of banking. The low cost of tracking large numbers of fast-circulating payments means that network technology can accelerate the velocity of money in such decentralized, microfinance programs. It is easy to imagine a high-yielding mutual fund based on hundreds of thousand of up-and-coming third world microentrepreneurs.

Third, the same type of fine-grained decentralization is about to happen in publicly traded companies. During the 1990s approximately 4,000 companies "went public" in the United States. These corporations were newly funded by the investment of many small shareholders, who collectively contributed about $250 billion to these companies' equity. Right now, very old-fashioned hurdles prevent many smaller companies from accepting equity investments by the public. Some of these hurdles are legacies from the industrial era when communication and information were scarce. Some obstacles are simply the selfish protections of investment bankers and others who reap billions by their monopoly on controlling the process of taking a company public. Network technology is radically altering the stock market, causing a widespread reevaluation of the role and worth of stock brokers, traders, and a centralized market itself (such as the New York Stock Exchange) in a world where economic information is ubiquitous and instant. Secure, reliable, and trustworthy offerings of publicly traded companies can happen on the net without most of the traditional Wall Street rigmarole. Network technology will make it possible for qualified companies to take their company public from a desktop, directly soliciting the investments from billions of individuals and organizations worldwide. This will happen sooner than Wall Street thinks.

Fourth, the Silicon Valley model of compensation is infecting more parts of the world. A major element of equity culture is the ideology that every person working in a company should have the opportunity to own part of it. In most American high-tech companies, stock options for employees are mandatory. Shares in the company are often used to recruit hot talent, or to be dispensed as bonuses, or, in the case of start-ups, to be paid out as a substitute for a salary. Companies that grant stock options to all employees return greater wealth to shareholders than companies that don't (19% for the former, 11% for the latter).

In the network economy, ownership is fragmented into myriad parts, sped along electronic pathways, and dispersed among workers, venture capitalists, investors, alliance members, outsiders, and, in minute doses, even to competitors. Networks breed swarm capitalism.

Yet as networks rise, the center recedes. It is no coincidence that global networks appear at the same time as the postmodern literary movement. In postmodernism, there is no central authority, no universal dogma, no foundational ethic. The theme of postmodernism in the arts, science, and politics is summed up by Steven Best and Douglas Kellner in their book *The Postmodern Turn:* "The postmodern turn results in fragmentation, instability, indeterminacy, and uncertainty." This also sums up the net.

Network principles renounce rigidity, closed structure, universal schemes, central authority, and fixed values. Instead networks offer up plurality, differences, ambiguity, incompleteness, contingency, and multiplicity. These qualities are ideal for disruption, for the spread of networked-organized crime, and for fostering the lack of shared values.

Because the nature of the network economy seeds disequilibrium, fragmentation, uncertainty, churn, and relativism, the anchors of meaning and value are in short supply. We are simply unable to deal with questions that cannot be answered by means of technology. The stereotypical modern consumer is already a rather thin character. He or she is like a balloon: possessing an inflated ego and a thin identity stretched to its limit. They don't know who they are, but they are very certain that they are very important. The smallest prick can pop their container.

In the great vacuum of meaning, in the silence of unspoken values, in the vacancy of something large to stand for, something bigger than one-self, technology—for better or worse—will shape our society.

Because values and meaning are scarce today, technology will make our decisions for us. We'll listen to technology because our modern ears listen to little else. In the absence of other firm beliefs, we'll let technology steer. No other force is as powerful in shaping our destiny. By imagining what technology wants, we can imagine the course of our culture.

The future of technology is networks. Networks large, wide, deep, and fast. Electrified networks of all types will cover our planet and their complex nodes will shape our economy and color our lives. The shift to this new perspective will be neither immediate nor painless. Nor will it be as strange as it first appears.

There is no reason to accept the imperative of technology without challenge, but there is also no doubt that technology's march is clearly aimed toward all things networked. Those who obey the logic of the net, and who understand that we are entering into a realm with new rules, will have a keen advantage in the new economy.

NEW RULES FOR THE NEW ECONOMY

1) **Embrace the Swarm.** As power flows away from the center, the competitive advantage belongs to those who learn how to embrace decentralized points of control.

2) **Increasing Returns.** As the number of connections between people and things add up, the consequences of those connections multiply out even faster, so that initial successes aren't self-limiting, but self-feeding.

3) **Plentitude, Not Scarcity.** As manufacturing techniques perfect the art of making copies plentiful, value is carried by abundance, rather than scarcity, inverting traditional business propositions.

4) **Follow the Free.** As resource scarcity gives way to abundance, generosity begets wealth. Following the free rehearses the inevitable fall of prices, and takes advantage of the only true scarcity: human attention.

5) **Feed the Web First.** As networks entangle all commerce, a firm's primary focus shifts from maximizing the firm's value to maximizing the network's value. Unless the net survives, the firm perishes.

6) **Let Go at the Top.** As innovation accelerates, abandoning the highly successful in order to escape from its eventual obsolescence becomes the most difficult and yet most essential task.

7) **From Places to Spaces.** As physical proximity (place) is replaced by multiple interactions with anything, anytime, anywhere (space), the opportunities for intermediaries, middlemen, and mid-size niches expand greatly.

8) **No Harmony, All Flux.** As turbulence and instability become the norm in business, the most effective survival stance is a constant but highly selective disruption that we call innovation.

9) **Relationship Tech.** As the soft trumps the hard, the most powerful technologies are those that enhance, amplify, extend, augment, distill, recall, expand, and develop soft relationships of all types.

10) **Opportunities Before Efficiencies.** As fortunes are made by training machines to be ever more efficient, there is yet far greater wealth to be had by unleashing the inefficient discovery and creation of new opportunities.

ACKNOWLEDGMENTS

This book benefited greatly from the work of researcher Jan Tudor, of JT Research in Portland, Oregon. Many people, including a number of qualified economists, supplied me with very helpful comments after reading the article upon which this book is based. These readers included Paul Romer, Paul Krugman, and George Gilder. Romer, Krugman, John Hagel, Paul Saffo, and Michael Kremer also provided interviews to me as well. A few other people took valuable time to read and comment on the manuscript version: John Heileman of *The New Yorker*, Russ Mitchell of *U.S. News & World Report*, Peter Schwartz of Global Business Network, and Hal Varian of the University of California, Berkeley. The fact-checking crew at *Wired* magazine made significant contributions, and as usual, saved me from embarrassment. At Viking, editor David Stanford turned my rough draft into a smooth piece of English while copy editor Danny Marcus further polished it to its present form. Many of the concepts expanded here originated in long conversations with John Perry Barlow, who was often the first to appreciate their power. John Brockman, my literary agent, saw a book in my ideas. My wife, Gia-Miin Fuh, sacrificed her weekends so I could write it; without that gift, this book wouldn't have happened. Thank you, all.

NOTES

4 **In DeLong's view:** DeLong's essay "Old Ideas for the New Economy," in *Rewired*, www.rewired.com.

8 **"Listen to the technology":** Quoted by George Gilder in the *Gilder Technology Report*, November 1996.

10 **a transistor cost:** "Happy 50th" by Heidi Elliott, in *Electronic Business*, December 1997.

10 **trillion objects manufactured:** Estimated by multiplying the estimated average number of objects one person buys in a year by the number of adults.

10 **200 million computers:** DataQuest.

10 **number of noncomputer chips:** DataQuest.

14 **Tree of Life:** http://phylogeny.arizona.edu/tree/phylogeny.html.

15 **GM saves $1.5 million:** "What Complexity Theory Can Teach Business" by David Berreby, in *Strategy & Business* Issue 3, 1996.

16 **a computer flight simulator:** This audience participation technology is operated by Cinematrix Interactive Entertainment Systems, Novato, CA, (415) 892-8254, or cies@nbn.com.

28 **"If a product":** "Increasing Returns and the New World of Business," by W. Brian Arthur, in *Harvard Business Review*, July 1996.

31 **"Technology is the campfire":** "Change is Good," *Wired*, January 1998.

36 **"the only reliable predictor":** "Chaos in Hollywood" by John Cassidy, in *The New Yorker*, March 31, 1997.

49 **Gilder's Law:** "Fiber Keeps Its Promise," by George Gilder, in *Forbes ASAP*, April 1997.

52 **"in the Network Economy":** "Entertainment Values: Will Capitalism Go Hollywood?" by Paul Krugman, in *Slate*, January 22, 1998.

55 **"What information consumes":** "The Information Economy" by Hal Varian, *Scientific American*, September 1995.

56 **first 1,000 days of the web's life:** Brewster Kahle's internet backup site www.archive.org.

59 **"The creator who":** "Intellectual Value" by Esther Dyson, in *Wired*, July 1995.

63 **"A web limits risk":** "Spider versus Spider" by John Hagel III, in *McKinsey Quarterly*, 1966 No. 1.

63 **"Players compete not by locking in":** "Increasing Returns and the New World of Business," by W. Brian Arthur, in *Harvard Business Review*, July 1996.

64 **in the 1890s, electricity:** "Computer and Dynamo" by Paul David, in *Technology and Productivity*, OECD, 1991.

68 **"Law is becoming irrelevant":** Quoted by David Brin in *The Transparent Society*, Addison-Wesley, 1998.

69 **boasted of an estimated 120 million:** Nua Ltd., May 1998.

69 **If current rates continue:** International Telecommunications Union 1998 Report.

71 **$212 billion on information:** Information Technology Industry Council.

72 **Rocky Mountain Institute:** Home page at www.rmi.org.

72 **electronics in a car:** "Ubiquitous Computing" by Sean Baenen at Global Business Network.

75 **"The time may come":** *Pop Internationalism*, by Paul Krugman, MIT Press, 1996.

80 **"Firms are remarkably creative":** *Mastering the Dynamics of Innovation*, by James M. Utterback, Harvard Business School Press, 1994.

83 **"Successful firms often":** "Recent Evolutionary Theorizing About Eco-

nomic Change," by Richard Nelson, in *Journal of Economic Literature*, March 1995.

85 **David Ackley:** "Interactions Between Learning and Evolution" by David H. Ackley and M. L. Littman, in *Artificial Life II*, edited by C. G. Langton, Addison-Wesley, 1992.

104 **the half-life of Texan businesses:** "A Nanaoeconomic Perspective on the Growth and Development of the Texas Manufacturing Base, 1970–1991," by Donald Hicks, in A Report Prepared for the Office of the Comptroller, State of Texas.

104 **the European Union:** "A Second American Century" by Mortimer B. Zuckerman, in *Foreign Affairs*, May/June 1998.

106 **"You're pitchforking a bunch of freelancers":** Bruce Sterling's speech at the 1998 Computers Freedom and Privacy Conference in Austin, Texas.

106 **entertainment complex:** "Why Every Business Will Be Like Show Business," by Joel Kotkin and David Friedman, in *Inc*, March 1995.

110 **"the Mecca of the economist":** Quoted by Richard Nelson, in "Recent Evolutionary Theorizing About Economic Change," by Richard Nelson, in *Journal of Economic Literature*, March 1995.

118 **an emerging standard called P3P:** Maintained by Firefly, www.firefly.net.

122 **sites such as Junglee or Jango:** www.junglee.com, www.jango.com.

125 **"the new economy begins":** "What's So New about the New Economy?" by Alan Weber, in *Harvard Business Review*, January/February 1993.

127 **"Whatever the Government":** "The Telephone Transformed—Into Almost Everything," by James Gleick, in *The New York Times Magazine*, May 16, 1993.

128 **protocols such as Truste:** www.truste.org.

134 **4 quadrillion dollars:** This rough guesstimate was extrapolated from the annual growth in the world's GDP. Since the economy grows about 1% annually, and that growth is 4 billion, the full size of the world's economy is close to a hundred times bigger, or 4 quadrillion.

134 **"Humans on average":** *The Ultimate Resource*, by Julian Simon, Princeton University Press, 1996.

137 **More than 320 million web pages:** Brewster Kahle's internet backup at www.archive.org.

139 **"Productivity isn't everything":** *The Age of Diminishing Expectations*, by Paul Krugman, MIT Press, 1994.

140 **a rise in productivity:** *The Rise of the Network Society*, by Manuel Castells, Blackwell Publishers, 1996.

141 **IBM alone sold:** "Mainframe Business, Though Faded, Is Still Far from Extinct" by Lawrence Fisher, *The New York Times*, May 18, 1998.

144 **"When a merchant sells a consumer":** *Unlimited Wealth*, by Paul Zane Pilzer, Crown Publishers, 1990.

145 **93% of Americans officially classified:** Quoting Federal Reserve Bank of Dallas economist Michael Cox, in an interview in "Wealth If You Want It," by Kevin Kelly, *Wired*, November 1996.

148–49 **28% of U.S. households:** "A Second American Century," by Mortimer B. Zuckerman, in *Foreign Affairs*, May/June 1998.

150 **"Lending to poor people":** "Credit where credit is due: Bringing microfinance into the mainstream," by Peter Montagnon, Center for the Study of Financial Innovation, February 1998.

ANNOTATED BIBLIOGRAPHY

The following books are ranked by relevance and degree of insight to understanding the new economy. This list starts with those I found most pertinent and ends with those that served as background. Left unlisted are many good books on economics and new business that contained only a few relevant ideas to this subject. Some of these additional resources are mentioned in my source notes. Following the annotated books is a list of useful web sites which have the best and most current material.

Information Rules: A Strategic Guide to the Network Economy, *by Carl Shapiro and Hal R. Varian. Harvard Business School Press, 1998.* If you want to go beyond the fundamental principles outlined in my book, try this one. This book is the best overview of the network economy yet, rigorously written by two bona fide economists, with careful analysis and plenty of real-life examples. Their emphasis is on high-tech and online environments, but their understanding is on target and widely applicable. Five stars.

Enterprise One to One: Tools for Competing in the Interactive Age, *by Don Peppers and Martha Rogers. Doubleday, 1997.* An excellent investigation into the future shape of relationships in the new economy. I learned all kinds of unexpected things from this well-written and witty book. It is very pragmatic about business tactics (how to get your company to interact with customers), but it also articulates useful economy principles at the strategic level as well. The authors seem to have an intuitive grasp of how the new economy is unfolding.

Net Gain: Expanding Markets Through Virtual Communities, *by John Hagel III and Arthur G. Armstrong. Harvard Business School Press, 1997.* A highly original and extremely insightful view of the new economy seen through the lens of commercial communities. It shifts focus away from firms or customers and onto emerging networks. It sees virtual communities as serious business. Although not economic in its sensibilities, this is one of the best books about the network economy. Highly recommended.

The Rise of the Network Society, *by Manuel Castells. Volume 1 of the Information Age. Blackwell Publishers, 1996.* A dense, sprawling, comprehensive vista of the ongoing transformation of society by network technologies. Castells is a sociologist with a European's bent for the large-scale sweep of history. This book, the first in a trilogy, is a catalog of evidence for the arrival of a new global, networked-based culture. The immense scope of this change is reflected in the immense, and at times unwieldy, scope of this book. Castells' literate and broad view is what makes it worthwhile.

Blur: The Speed of Change in the Connected Economy, *by Stan Davis and Christopher Meyer. Addison-Wesley, 1998.* Further explorations of the consequences of the network economy. The authors list three primary forces overturning the old order: speed, intangibles, and connectivity (which parallel my three of globalization, intangibles, and connectivity). They have lots of business examples and yet more strategies.

Unleashing the Killer App: Digital Strategies for Market Dominance, *by Larry Downes and Chunka Mui. Harvard Business School Press, 1998.* Despite the slightly misleading title, this book celebrates the network economy. It arrives at similar conclusion as I do, and it even has its own list of new rules (on page 77). However, its focus is on the practical creation of a business service or product in the new economy. It is not as methodical or complete as *Information Rules*, but I think it is a good general businessperson's introduction.

Webonomics, *by Evan I. Schwartz. Broadway Books, 1997.* Schwartz focuses very specifically on the practical problems of using web sites to create commerce. His nine principles for doing business on the web won't hold true for the entire new economy, but they are pointed in the right direction. If you are running a commercial web site, his advice is certainly helpful.

The Digital Estate: Strategies for Competing, Surviving, and Thriving in an Internetworked World, *by Chuck Martin. McGraw-Hill, 1996.* A super book for getting a feel for the new online business culture. Martin gives you a visceral sense of the tremendous cleverness, brilliant innovations, and experimental business models happening "out of sight" on the web. He's a great tour guide to this strange new territory, and the best way to get a sense of "what's happening" in online commerce.

The Economics of Electronic Commerce, *by Andrew B. Whinston, Dale O. Stahl, and Soon-Yong Choi. Macmillan Technical Publishing, 1997.* Electronic commerce is barely born and already has its textbook. This one is a pretty good textbook, too. The material is wonderfully interdisciplinary, covering economics, engineering, finance, and marketing. In addition to the usual papers and book references, the authors also list plenty of relevant web site urls. For doing business online, this textbook is better than having an MBA.

The Digital Economy: Promise and Peril in the Age of Networked Intelligence, *by Don Tapscott. McGraw-Hill, 1996.* In a not very organized fashion, this book wanders through some of the emerging dynamics of the network economy. There are lots of examples of new economy business, but with little theory, and a minimum of analysis. Overall, he is good at picking out new economy business trends.

Electronic Commerce: A Manager's Guide, by Ravi Kalakota and Andrew B. Whinston. Addison-Wesley, 1997. One of those books that are very timely at the moment, but will date quickly. Here is everything known in 1997 about managing electronic commerce on a web site. How to do firewalls, transaction security, and electronic payments from the view of a nonprogramming mid-level manager. If the authors are smart, they'll keep this tome updated.

The Weightless World: Strategies for Managing the Digital Economy, by Diane Coyle. Capstone Publishing, 1997. This book, unlike many of the others listed here, is more concerned with the economic consequences, rather than the business implications, of the new economy. Coyle begins to grapple with the issues such as welfare, governance, and policy decisions which a "weightless" world of information will demand. Another way of saying this is that Coyle often considers the downsides of the new economy. Such questioning is sorely needed.

Release 2.0: A Design for Living in the Digital Age, by Esther Dyson. Broadway Books, 1997. A pretty good primer aimed at lay people explaining the social consequences of network society and culture. Covers a full range of topics from privacy to identity to communities and intellectual property. Sort of like a orientation tour of this exotic tomorrowland.

The Age of the Network: Organizing Principles for the 21st Century, by Jessica Lipnack and Jeffrey Stamps. Oliver Wright Publications, 1994. Despite its very new-agey tone, this book is useful as a background. It combines the understanding of everyday social networks with the understanding of electronic networks to provide some key insights into how human networks in general work. And it makes clear their increasing influence.

Bionomics: Economy as Ecosystem, by Michael Rothschild. Henry Holt and Company, 1990. A chatty amplification of a very fundamental metaphor—the economy behaves like a ecosystem. Buried in the stories about trilobites and bacteria, are some very keen insights about the network economy.

The Death of Competition: Leadership and Strategy in the Age of Business Ecosystems, by James F. Moore. HarperCollins, 1996. The closest analogy to a network is an ecosystem. Moore plumbs the biological metaphor in great detail and with more success, perhaps, than Bionomics does. I consider these ideas prime territory still waiting to be exploited. This book is a good start.

The Economy as an Evolving Complex System, edited by Philip W. Anderson, Kenneth J. Arrow, and David Pines. Addison-Wesley, 1988. The published proceedings from a landmark workshop on ecological approaches to deciphering the economy. Very technical and academic, but also very revolutionary.

Increasing Returns and Path Dependence in the Economy, by W. Brain Arthur. University of Michigan Press, 1994. If you are willing to try unprocessed originals, the papers in this collection can illuminate the key and pivotal function of increasing returns. Written by the economist who coined the term, at least some of the papers are accessible and clear to lay readers.

The Winner-Take-All Society, by Robert H. Frank and Philip J. Cook. Penguin Books, 1995. Since there is a winner-take-most element to the network economy, this readable book-length essay is quite provocative.

Internet Economics, edited by Lee W. McKnight and Joseph P. Bailey. MIT Press, 1997. A well-chosen selection of scholarly papers outlining the economic problems created by internet commerce. Most questions in the compendium deal with the baffling problem of how to price services in a distributed environment. How should shared connections, or insurance, or occasional links be priced? How should traffic be regulated? What shape will money take? This is the engineer's approach to economics.

The Death of Distance: How the Communications Revolution Will Change Our Lives, by Frances Cairncross. Harvard Business School Press, 1997. An accurate book, but with the thin and well-worn announcement that global communications are changing the world. Low on surprises or insight, but full of facts.

The Self-Organizing Economy, by Paul Krugman. Blackwell Publishers, 1996. A slim volume of fairly technical descriptions of how decentralized, bottom-up self-organization can shape some economic phenomenon, such as cities.

The Future of Money in the Information Age, edited by James A. Dorn. Cato Institute, 1997. Money, which is a type of information, is changing as fast as the economy it circulates in. This is an academic view of how money and financial institutions are transforming.

Digital Money: The New Era of Internet Commerce, by Daniel Lynch and Leslie Lundquist. John Wiley & Sons, 1996. Lynch, a founder of a digital cash system, paints a portrait of the new economy as viewed from the perspective of liquid, intangible e-money. The shape of money in the future is a huge, vital, and unknown question, one that I skirted for space reasons. This book is a great place to catch up.

Cybercorp: The New Business Revolution, by James Martin. Amacon, 1996. Martin is a legendary telecom guru who has written over a hundred books. This one is a jumble of buzz words, astounding insights, tired clichés, astute musings, interesting graphs, corny lessons, wonderful statistics, lame explanations, and bubbly enthusiasm. He's often right, and he is focused on the new economy, but the reader will have to do the winnowing.

The Twilight of Sovereignty, by Walter B. Wriston. Charles Scribner's Sons, 1992. Not as revolutionary as it was when it was first published in 1992, this short book still makes a very intelligible case for a new economy birthing. Wriston pays particular attention to the geopolitical impacts of a networked information economy.

Shared Minds: New Technologies of Collaboration, *by Michael Schrage. Random House, 1990.* Although not explicitly about networks or network technology, this book is about what happens when you use tools—such as networks—to create collaborations of minds, for both work and play. It is more about the future of business organization than most books advertised as such.

Regional Advantage: Culture and Competition in Silicon Valley and Route 128, *by Annalee Saxenian. Harvard University Press, 1994.* A wonderful book about the success of network culture in Silicon Valley, brought into relief by comparing it to the older, but less successful and less networked, high-tech culture based in the vicinity of Boston.

Innovation Explosion, *by James Brian Quinn, Jordan J. Baruch, and Karen Anne Zien. The Free Press, 1997.* If knowledge is the new capital, then innovation is the new currency. Quinn and colleagues do a masterful job of placing innovation as the central dynamic in a knowledge economy. They have rounded up anecdotes, statistics, and bullet points galore to create a believable case for why innovation is the key variable in the network economy.

Post-Capitalistic Society, *by Peter Drucker. HarperCollins, 1993.* An early picture of the coming new economy which has not aged a bit. Drucker is always worth reading.

Unlimited Wealth: The Theory and Practice of Economic Alchemy, *by Paul Zane Pilzer. Crown Publishers, 1990.* This one is an outlier, a little on the extreme side. More than most observers, Pilzer is not hesitant to speculate on the ways in which technology increases prosperity in an economy. His heretical ideas are refreshing.

The Third Wave, *by Alvin Toffler. Bantam, 1980.* A classic, and yet still incredibly up-to-date and informative. Toffler's 20-year-old profile of a new economy and new culture is more readable and more accurate than most depictions written since.

New Ideas from Dead Economists: An Introduction to Modern Economic Thought, *by Todd G. Buchholz. Penguin Books, 1990.* Most "new" ideas in economics, as in everything else, are not new at all. This compact volume is the best one-stop shop for extracting the best thoughts of previous economists. Painless and edifying, this text should be in every network economist's library.

The Information Economy. *http://www.sims.berkeley.edu/resources/ infoecon/* The most complete web site for the new economy. This clear, wide-ranging, and very up-to-date site, run by economist Hal Varian, coauthor of *Information Rules* (see above), lists papers, works in process, and hundreds of links to other new economy sites. Almost any web site that is remotely connected to the information or network economy is linked here, including, for example, the follow two sites.

George Gilder's Telecosm Index. *http://homepage.seas.upenn.edu/~gaj1/ ggindex.html* Chapters of author George Gilder's epic book-in-progress on the emerging telecommunications universe are archived here. Gilder's thinking is seminal, and many of my own rules owe much to him. Keep an eye out for his book *Telecosm*, due out in late 1998; until then, these articles from *Forbes* are a real goldmine.

The Economics of Networks. *http://raven.stern.nyu.edu/networks/site.html* This site is primarily dedicated to examining the economic implications of communication networks. It is crammed with papers by the site organizer (economist Nicholas Economides), but also includes a very handy bibliography and master list of all other economists working on the economics of networks.

INDEX

Page numbers in *italics* refer to charts and figures.

ABOUT THE AUTHOR

Kevin Kelly is executive editor of *Wired* magazine. In 1993 and 1996, under his co-editorship, *Wired* won its industry's Oscar—the National Magazine Award for General Excellence. Prior to the launch of *Wired*, Kelly was editor/publisher of the *Whole Earth Review*, a journal of unorthodox technical and cultural news. His previous book is *Out of Control: The New Biology of Machines, Social Systems and the Economic World*, a book about a new paradigm for technology. The text of *Out of Control* and other material can be found on his homepage: http://www.well.com/user/kk. The best way to reach him is via email: kk@well.com.